SHAD
TIGER COUNTRY

Life is short. Enjoy every second.

SHADOW IN
TIGER COUNTRY

One Last Year of Love

—

Louise & Tim Arthur

HarperCollins*Publishers*

HarperCollins*Publishers*
77–85 Fulham Palace Road,
Hammersmith, London w6 8jb

www.**fire**and**water**.com

Published by HarperCollins*Publishers* 2000
1 3 5 7 9 8 6 4 2

Copyright © Tim Arthur 2000

The Authors assert their moral right to
be identified as the authors of this work

A catalogue record for this book
is available from the British Library

ISBN 0 00 653242 X

Set in ITC New Baskerville by
Rowland Phototypesetting Ltd,
Bury St Edmunds, Suffolk

Printed and bound in Great Britain by
Omnia Books Limited, Glasgow

For CAITLIN

Prologue

In January 1999, Louise began the diary on her website.

When I was fifteen I spent about six months in bed with a vague, undiagnosed condition described at the time as a post-viral infection by my GP. In retrospect I think this was a symptom of my condition, although it was not diagnosed for another nine years. From the age of eighteen I suffered from pretty appalling headaches and turned to alternative medicine for the answer, having had little help from my then GP. I was treated by acupuncturists, homeopaths, osteopaths, nutritionists, reflexologists, aromatherapists and various spiritual healers. No one suggested I had a brain scan or even intimated that they might not be able to sort out the headaches. During this time I was vegetarian and did copious amounts of yoga and T'ai Chi. I also spent a great deal of time searching for a reason within myself or on some spiritual level as to why I was in pain.

In 1993 I fell dramatically in love with Tim, who proposed two days after we first kissed. We were married three months later and are still blissfully in love. In November '95 we had Caitlin, our gorgeous little girl. During the pregnancy I developed Horner's Syndrome (a drooping eyelid), so when Caitlin was six weeks old I had a brain scan. What it showed was a very large 'shadow' in my sphenoid sinus in the centre of my head. I had a biopsy soon afterwards. A week before the biopsy results were due the hospital phoned at 8 a.m. and asked me to come in. I overheard the surgeon asking a nurse to 'come in while I tell her', and at that point I knew I had a malignant tumour.

He told me it was slow growing and I had had it for years – also that it was very likely to be inoperable as it was in 'tiger country'. A couple of weeks later I met a fantastic surgeon, Professor Gleeson, and after a load of tests and scans he and a brain surgeon called Mr Strong did a twelve-hour operation to 'debulk' the tumour. After some recovery time I had a very intensive course of radiotherapy and chemotherapy.

That was all two years ago. I made a fantastic recovery, discovered photography, made a darkroom in our house, rediscovered all the important things in life and generally assumed I had learnt what I could from the experience of having cancer, that I was a happier, more fulfilled person and that I was in remission. I wrote in an article for *Marie Claire* magazine 'I think the cancer has given me more than it has taken away . . .'

Just after Christmas I lost feeling in the right side of my face. At first I thought it might just be the result of a bad cold

I had had recently, but when it hadn't gone after a few days I rang up my GP, who told me to go back to Guy's. After a meeting with Professor Gleeson again I was in no real doubt that the cancer had returned (or rather, never really gone away), but when I went for my scan results meeting I was expecting to discuss chemotherapy dates. What actually happened was that Professor Gleeson met Tim and me and took us into his office as opposed to his consulting room and told us, in a very caring and clear way, that I was going to die. He showed us the scans and told us that there were one or two people he could talk to if we wanted him to about the possibility of treatment of some kind. However, preliminary enquiries he had made indicated that no one thought they could do much more than slightly extend my life, and that at great cost to my health.

My memories of chemotherapy were not good, to say the least, so we decided to see if anyone thought they could help, but to reserve the right to decline if it looked too painful. In the event there was only one doctor who thought he might be able to do something and after he saw the scans he decided he couldn't. The tumour is currently residing in the main vein in my head (which makes surgery impractical) and around the back of my nose (which is somewhat bloody). My face (well, half of it) is still numb, but I am in no pain and do not look any different.

I am rather deaf on my right side – although strangely enough the ticking of clocks I find almost unbearably loud.

This was what Louise (or Weeze, as I called her) put up by way of a background page on her website which was to be a diary of her last year of life. I'm not sure when we started out on the extraordinary journey that the last year was to be that either of us had any idea what it would really be like to go through such a traumatic experience. Her tone seems very jolly, very upbeat, and writing this as I am only a few days after she has died it seems almost ridiculous to imagine that we could even try to document such a tragedy. But that was Weeze, she was and is one of the most positive people I have ever come across. Not blindly positive though, and indeed in the last few months her moods swung desperately from despair to elation, but as you'll read from her diary she managed to find things from this terrible disease which gave her an insight into life and living which few people ever gain.

Louise always wanted to be a writer – the people she most admired were writers, poets and artists – and her diary was really her last chance to join the ranks of those that so enriched her life. As with all of us, she always thought she had time to do things later, a novel perhaps or a collection of poetry or something. She had an artistic spirit and in her final year she blossomed. Nothing focuses the mind like a deadline, I guess. She wrote and wrote, and took up photography with remarkable results and basically knuckled down to working. Without the cancer I'm convinced she could have spent the rest of her life saying 'I must get round to writing something soon'. As it was she was desperate to get everything out of her. For the first time in her life she felt like she had something to say, things she wanted to communicate to people, and indeed she did. This book contains some of that, something of her, but not all of her, of course. We were interviewed by the *Independent* about Louise's website a few months before she died and the lady interviewing us over the phone asked me, 'What one thing will you most miss about Louise, Tim?' At the time I remember wanting to throttle her for such a stupid question, but I took a few deep breaths and said, 'There's not one thing, it's all of her, it's every single thing of the billions of things which make her what she is that I'll miss.' And that's still the truth. And with this book it will only give the reader the tiniest insight into who she really was, but that's good in a way because that means that there's lots of her that's still mine and not for public consumption.

Why write the book? Good question. Louise always wanted to write a book, and when she started the diary she always hoped that one day it might get published. So when the nice people at HarperCollins approached us about writing a book Louise was over the moon. I remember her dancing around the kitchen then getting dizzy and falling into a chair laughing. 'I can't believe it – a book, a book! And they want you to write half of it, can you believe it?' It made me laugh that she was so excited about sharing the project. She loved sharing things. At the time when we were planning the book it was going to be somewhat different to the way it has turned out now. It was going to be less a book based round the diary and more a book led by subjects which have come to the fore in our lives since Louise was diagnosed. It was going to be a book about us, our lives, our love, the cancer, being parents and loads of other stuff. Louise was very interested in the reactions her illness caused and how people responded to us, from religious friends who set up prayer groups, some of our younger friends who cut themselves off from us and we haven't seen since she was first diagnosed, and a thousand other responses, some lovely, some less so. She also wanted people to start talking about death and dying – she hated the taboo nature of the disease. She couldn't believe that people still referred to it as the

Big C or called it 'It', as if merely saying the word cancer would somehow give it power.

She also wanted to shake people out of complacency. Life is about living and she couldn't bear to see people wasting their lives, or whingeing about them. 'Life's too short not to be doing something you love,' she would often be found saying over dinner to any number of our friends who had simply mentioned in passing that they weren't quite as fulfilled at work as they might like to be. Her illness made her reckless with her evangelical advice. She was unafraid of telling people to change, to take control of their lives, and several people we knew ended up leaving their jobs and even partners after a particularly good session with Weeze. This wasn't to say that she wasn't kind and gracious and understanding, because she was all of these things, which meant that when she told you something you tended to listen more readily and really take it to heart.

Unfortunately, just a few days after we'd negotiated the contract for the book, Louise's condition took a turn for the worse. What we'd at first envisaged the book to be became impossible. There was no way as she got weaker and weaker that she could write and the mental energy needed to talk thought the issues made it harder and harder. Eventually it became clear that Louise's input to the book would mainly be entries from the diary she'd already written, with me fleshing out some of the issues with a kind of commentary. So this is what I'm going to do. I only hope I can do justice to her, but we'll have a go.

Before we start I'd just like to say one thing about Weeze. She was no saint. This isn't an account of a perfect woman, whose noble heart and pure soul brought light into the world. Weeze was a funny, strong, beautiful lady who made my whole life worth living, but I'm not going to idolize her or put her up on a pedestal. She would have hated that, so I promise I'll try to be as honest as I can be. It may sometimes be painful and sometimes I'm sure I'll fail, but as I set out it's important that I intend to tell it as it was and is. If we are to learn anything from our experiences it's important that we are truthful about them and the things that happened. Having said that, even now I can feel my mind working overtime trying to rewrite and alter the images of the last few months to protect me, so I'll write fast and try to get everything down before Time the great healer begins to mess around with my already unreliable memory.

Chapter 1

In the summer of 1993 I was a svelte – well, OK, not quite svelte, but not as big as I was to become with Louise's excellent cooking – long-haired recent graduate. As I looked out on to my future life it all seemed clouded in an exciting mystery. I started working with a group of local misfits in a comedy impro outfit called 'The Bucket Cabaret'. Each week we'd spend hours sitting round drinking wine and lager, trying to come up with more and more ludicrous sketches. Naked chefs, freakish gameshow hosts, twisted rappers, became part and parcel of my everyday life. We played to audiences of varying size and varying enthusiasm. There were, however, some devoted regulars, most of whom knew or were going out with someone in the show. Louise was one of these. Her ex-boyfriend Lewis was one of the performers and because of him mainly she came down to lend support.

This quiet, shy, pretty lady always sat somewhere near the front and always smiled rather than laughed out loud.

I'd known her vaguely for years. When we were fifteen or so she'd been on the other side of the group of friends I hung out with. She was at that time a Goth chick who dressed in black make-up, short skirts and fishnet stockings that attempted to hide her magnificent long legs. She always scared me – she was a woman with older men for boyfriends up in London, while I was a geeky guy whose whole life revolved around a very poor rock band and playing various Shakespearean characters in school plays. Whenever I spoke to Weeze then I got tongue tied, felt incredibly short and ugly, and was generally relieved when it was over, although I fancied her more than any other girl in our town. Funny how we perceive ourselves. I was always convinced that she didn't really like me. She later told me that she was just shy and that she saw me as this confident pop singer – she liked me, but as I always had a girlfriend she never thought it was worth pursuing. Not that she fancied me at all, as she would often say during our relationship. 'I didn't fancy Tim at all until we kissed then I instantly fell in love with him.' It's a strange backwards compliment. On the bad side she hadn't fancied me, on the good side it must have been some kiss.

So let me tell you about the kiss. After one of the shows, Louise invited the whole team back to her house for an after-show soirée. We all sat round in the kitchen and I made a shameful attempt to impress. Over the past few weeks I'd been talking to her ex about all the things she liked, from books and films to music and behaviour in men. That night I used all my accrued knowledge to win her over. Whatever subject came up, I made sure I was the first to speak about it, saying exactly what I thought she'd like to hear. 'Ian McEwan is probably the finest writer of our time.' 'Wasn't punk a fantastic period for music?' 'You know what, I may be weird but I love ironing and hate watching sport on telly.' After half an hour or so, Weeze looked across at me and said, 'Should we just go upstairs now?'

I was convinced this transparent ploy would fail miserably but it worked a treat. Perhaps because most of the things were true – nearly every book I had ever read and loved so did she, nearly all the films that formed my early mind had had a similar effect on Weeze. OK, the ironing and sports stuff was rubbish, but you've got to go with what you feel. Just after two in the morning I thought it was time I should be going and I made a move for the door. Weeze said she'd walk me out and as we stood – corny as it was – in the moonlight of the front path, I leant forward to kiss her goodnight. What should have been a quick peck on the cheek became one of those embarrassing missed kisses where both thought the other was going for the other cheek and end up actually kissing on the lips. Now, what should have been the briefest of kisses lasted possibly only a millisecond longer than would have been decent, but it was enough. It was enough to make us both pull back in surprise. I started to stutter and stammer and Louise just smiled. I ran all the way home and jumped into bed and spent a restless night wondering what on earth to do.

Next morning I got up early, as I was meant to be leaving for a male bonding trip with one of my best friends, Ben, around Britain. Before I went, though, I thought it was only right and proper to go round and apologize for the previous night's indiscretion. On the off-chance I might get a similar indiscretion. I found a CD we'd both mentioned the night before, *Thank You World* by World Party, and thought this would be a good excuse. As I knocked on her front door I could see her bounding her way downstairs in a pair of leggings and a very small tight white t-shirt. I would later find out that she'd put this on specifically on the off-chance that I might turn up, as the night before I mentioned something about liking tight t-shirts on women with great breasts. Well, who doesn't? She opened the door and I started jabbering on.

'About last night, I'm really sorry, I mean I'm just, you know, I'm not sure what happened, I'm just, I shouldn't have done it. Well, I mean I'm not sorry it happened, it was very nice and everything, it's just, I mean, I'm sorry if you didn't like it.'

If I'd been two feet taller, a lot better looking and had an upper class accent I could have been Hugh Grant, such was my fumbling incoherence. She leant forward and kissed me, I think as much to shut me up as anything, and we kissed and we kissed. Quite unbelievably, we kissed for three hours in her corridor and in her kitchen. Half-way through she told me she had a friend upstairs who she'd been doing T'ai Chi with when the doorbell rang. 'Do you think it would be rude if we went upstairs and had sex, while he's in the next room?' she asked. We agreed it probably was and, besides, I really had to go. I gave her my bracelet as a keepsake and I left.

'I can't believe I only just found you, and now I've got to leave,' came out of my mouth from absolutely nowhere and I think that was the line that finally did it. She would repeat that line to me over our whole marriage as being one of the sweetest things anyone had ever said to her. Well, it's nice to know that out of the million and one crap things that came out of my mouth over our relationship, at least I said something right.

When I got back from my week-long voyage of discovery around the British Isles I headed over to see Louise. She opened the door, dragged me in, straight upstairs and I emerged three days later in a state of ecstatic bliss and engaged.

Basically for those three days we did nothing but drink champagne, make love and massage each other. In fact, it was during one of these massage sessions that we had our magic experience. Now, I am fully prepared to accept that whatever happened could have been due to lack of sleep, exhaustion and alcohol, but I should say that I believe it to be one of the only true experiences that has ever happened to me. I'll describe it for you and those of you with a New Age spiritual bent can read all sorts of things into it. Those of you with a more objective point of view may see it in a different way. Anyway, what happened was this: we entered Louise's massage room – she was an aromatherapist at the time – and as we got naked we slowly massaged each other, until it felt as if touching each other was too much to take and we began to massage each other's auras. Then it happened. I felt my heart chakra open, as did Louise, and something left my chest and passed into her and something from her came and joined with me. We sat there in silence for the longest time, unable to talk or verbalize the experience. It was the middle of the night before we managed to leave the room and went and lay holding each other in bed. I can remember saying, 'Wow, if this isn't love then I don't know what is. And I don't think I could take it if there's anything more intense than this. I think that's it. I think we've found each other. I think we should get married.'

This didn't phase Weeze at all. She just nodded and said, 'Yes, I think you're right. Maybe we should just check it with the I Ching.'

For anyone who doesn't know, the I Ching is a Chinese form of divination, which helps you to look into the future. Basically, you flip a coin six times and depending which way it lands each time will help you build up a hexagram, which you then look up in a book for some words of wisdom. We did this and it came up as the I Ching H'sien, which our book simply said was 'beautiful marriage'. Considering none of the other hexagrams mention marriage and a lot of them are downright depressing, this was enough of a sign. I got out of bed and knelt on one knee, naked, and proposed. She giggled and simply said, 'Let's.' We kissed and made love again and that was it, the deal was done, and three months later we were married.

As I read through all that, it seems like a ridiculous dream. Why on earth we were so certain it would work, I've no idea. It was just right, and that was it. I remember talking to Louise's father about the wedding – this being the first time he'd met me – and he wasn't at all phased but simply asked us whether or not we would mind waiting just a few more months so that he could get some money together to help us. At the time I thought he was mad, didn't he get it, this was love, this was real passion, of course we couldn't wait, we had to get married straight away. Now, though, I look back on it and wonder how he didn't just look at me and say, 'You've got to be kidding. You've only really known each other three or four days and you want to get married in three months. Are you crazy?' But he didn't say that and when we said we couldn't wait he accepted it and I was one of the family, a family I'm very privileged to be in.

The wedding was a blast (but more of that later) and the honeymoon in Egypt was a fiasco on near biblical scale (but again more of that later). Over the next couple of years we packed a lot in. I managed to have a nervous breakdown after we lost a baby very early in the pregnancy, then Louise found out she had endometriosis and went through a series of operations and we were told we might never have children. But after all that was behind us we got pregnant, or rather, Louise got pregnant with some help from me. A thousand and one things went through my mind over the first few months of the pregnancy. Will I be a good father? Should I be strict or soppy? Do I want a boy or a girl? Boys can play rugby, but girls are cuter. That sort of thing. The one thing that didn't occur to me was what if my wife discovers she has cancer just a month after our daughter is born?

Louise was incredibly sick all through the pregnancy, throwing up eight or nine times a day, and very nearly got taken into hospital several times because of dehydration. For the first five months or so, she was more or less bedridden. Far from gaining weight, she lost it, and as her little belly filled out the rest of her got thinner and thinner. I had a play at the Edinburgh Festival in August of that year and miraculously she got better for the week we were up there, but almost as soon as we were home again she was back to the sick bucket, which in our house was a silver champagne cooler. As Louise said, 'If you've got to be sick into something, it might as well be nice.'

The sickness gradually subsided, though, as we entered the third trimester and it was about that time that Louise got her drooping eyelid. It started off as a slight thing that only happened when she was particularly tired and I think at the time all of us presumed it was something to do with the traumatic times she'd had over the last few months. We went to see our doctor and he referred us to a specialist. We sat there and he looked Louise over and told her she had this thing called Horner's Syndrome. I can remember all the tests he did very clearly, mainly because I would see them repeated over and over again by many many different doctors over the next few months and years. She was asked to follow his finger as it moved around the periphery of her vision, he lightly touched her skin with a piece of cotton wool to test for sensitivity, he looked into her eyes with one of those torch things. All in all it went on for some time and did nothing to ease our minds. At the end of it he said he'd quite like Louise to have a scan soon after the baby was born as they couldn't do it before because it might hurt the child. I remember asking him in a jovial manner, 'It's not a brain tumour or anything is it?' I smiled at my over-dramatic and paranoid question. And then he said, and I'll never forget this, 'No, in all the cases I've seen of Horner's Syndrome over the last twenty years not one of them has been caused by a tumour.' Well, you know, you win some, you lose some.

Two months or so later, Caitlin was born. What a birth that was! It all started off badly because we hadn't prepared at all, so when Louise woke me up one morning to tell me she'd gone into labour I could still hear in my head our ante-natal tutor telling us 'Make sure you've packed your bags well in advance of the birth date, just in case.' Well, it was a couple of weeks after our due date and we hadn't even thought about the bag. So we ran around like blue-arsed flies trying to gather all the stuff we needed. As is my wont in times of need, I headed for the fridge. All I could remember was that it might take a long time and a packed lunch was recommended. Louise came into the kitchen as her second contraction hit her. 'Oof, there's another one. You know what though, it's not too bad.' Off she wandered to find something or other and I delved back into the fridge for the ingredients of a Scooby Snack size sandwich. I saw Louise coming towards me down the corridor when her next contraction struck, only this time it was somewhat more powerful. In fact, it was powerful enough to floor her. The thump was loud enough to spook our cat, who bolted out of the cat-flap.

'I knew it was going to hurt,' she screamed, 'but not this fucking much.'

It was then I realized that we were in for a bumpy ride. Louise grew up in a family where swearing is considered to show a lack of vocabulary, while in my family swearing isn't even considered, it's just what we do. Not that much, you understand, I don't want to give you the impression that my folks are foul-mouthed in any way, it's just that we can swear if we have to, with marvellous aplomb and panache. The point is, if Louise was swearing, it meant it really hurt.

We rushed off to hospital and after driving the wrong way for twenty minutes I eventually worked out where we were meant to be going, turned the car round and arrived there just in time to be told to go home for a few hours.

'You're hardly dilated at all, go home, have a bath and take some paracetamol,' the sadistic midwife said.

'Will the paracetamol help?' a desperate-looking Weeze asked.

'No, not really.' And on that happy note we headed off for home.

It was whilst back at home that I made one of the biggest

mistakes of my marriage. I put Louise in the bath and phoned up my dad to tell him we were on our way. He then came over. It was at this point that I thought it might be nice for posterity's sake to get a photographic record of the birth. In her writhing agony Louise didn't put up any particular objection to this. However, when the photos came back from the chemist two weeks later she was somewhat stunned at quite how intimate these pictures were. She was particularly gobsmacked when she realized that I was actually in half the pictures, holding my naked wife's hand. 'But, Tim, if you're in this picture, who took them?' For some reason knowing that they'd been taken by the man who'd been responsible for me being in the world didn't appease her at all.

Anyway, when we eventually got back into the hospital the contractions were coming thick and fast and Louise's howling was getting worse with every one. It's strange how horribly useless you feel at times like this, times of pain and desperation, but I kept reminding myself and her that this was a good pain. Something I would have given anything to be able to tell her four years later. Weeze had always said she fancied trying to have the baby naturally without any anaesthetic. A neighbour of ours, Dorothy, heard about this a few days before Louise went into labour and said, 'Why on earth would you do that? You wouldn't have your leg cut off without anaesthetic.' As it turned out, she had a good point. Louise put up with the pain for eight heroic hours and then eventually screamed for an epidural. I reminded her of her previous convictions and she looked at me with dagger eyes. So I called in the nurse and we got her nicely drugged up.

After this it was all plain sailing, we put some mellow music on and she still managed to push the baby out on her own. By 9 p.m. in the evening I was holding my little girl. Holding her like a cracked egg I expected to break at any moment, but holding her nevertheless, and I fell in love. I fell in love with this warm, snuffling creature in my arms and I fell in love all over again with my exhausted, serene wife. I was and still am in awe of the sheer ordeal that childbirth is. It is amazing, frightening and un-believably exhilarating. I was one of those men who was flipped upside down by the whole experience. Watching Weeze feed Caitlin for the first time is an image that is somehow seared on to my soul. It was one of those moments that moulds and forms you into the person you become after it. From that second onwards your life changes, you go from being a boy and girl into a mum and dad. It's a big step, bigger than anything Neil Arm-strong took. Well, it blew me away, anyway. And then we were three, and at that time I still thought we'd be three for ever. But that wasn't to be. There were other events about to enter our lives which would shatter our world.

We faced everything, we got through the twelve-hour operation, we got through the numerous treatments, Weeze even managed to kick her addiction to the heroin-like painkiller she'd been put on, we got through it all. And what's more, we'd laughed, danced, hugged, made love, watched our child grow up and start school, and then it came back. Only this time there was nothing we could do about it. Our surgeon, Professor Gleeson, one of the most lovely men I've ever met, had to tell us both that that was it, there was nothing more anyone could do. We walked out of his office, walked down the corridor, walked down to London Bridge station, sat in a bar, quickly knocked back a brandy, went on to the platform, held each other, sobbed, then got on the train home, back to our daughter, our family, with the kind of news that is as painful to pass on as it is to receive.

Chapter 2

—

There was a strange sense of relief that went with the horror of the news. Every time we went up for one of the meetings every four months or so, both of us felt sick and nervous. We'd spend the hour-long train journey torturing ourselves about the best or worst case scenarios. But that day had surpassed anything we'd come up with. We suspected it was bad, that we were facing more chemo or radiotherapy. But Prof told us we had a year to a year and a half and that we should go off and try to enjoy the time we had left as much as we possibly could. And that's exactly what we did.

We spent very little time feeling sorry for ourselves. We concentrated mainly on the things we wanted to do and how we wanted to achieve them. Louise wanted to travel a bit, which meant I had to get over my fear of flying, and she wanted to have some special days eating in restaurants she loved, wearing nice clothes, spend as much time with Caitlin as she could and, perhaps more difficult to achieve, she wanted to make her mark. Leave something behind that would be a lasting epitaph to who she was. It was about this time that we hit on the idea of the Internet diary. I had become an Internet convert several months before. One of our best friends, Gavin, had just started designing websites, Louise had always been fascinated by diaries and so we all put our heads together and came up with 'Shadow Diary – a diary of terminal cancer'. Weeze was very specific about what she wanted from the site: she wanted it to be a place where she could vent her spleen and give an honest account of how she was feeling at each and every stage of her illness. She also wanted a place where she could exhibit her photographs and a place where others could come to talk about the illness and start a kind of web community. I think she achieved everything she'd hoped and a little more. By the time she died her website had had somewhere in the region of 300,000 hits and it still continues to go up daily.

She kept it up nearly every day and, as you'll see, it became her way of sorting through what was going on in her own head. She was over-protective of me in many ways and so used the diary like a counsellor or a partner to chat things through with. She would examine things inside it that she didn't want me to have to face, a thing I regret a little. Although we talked a lot and got through the experience together, I know there were bits of her that were frightened and anxious, bits which I let her keep inside or sometimes let her tell the whole world on the Net rather than talk to me. That may be why I rarely read the diary while she was alive. The things she wrote in her diary were the things her internal voice was saying, and I was afraid it would be too painful too handle. I couldn't bear to know the mental torture that she felt at times. Physical pain I could handle, there were things I could do about that – I could call doctors in, I could give her more morphine – but sometimes I didn't want to know where she was in her head, I couldn't handle it. Weeze was my rock. I needed her to be strong and there for me, I couldn't think of her not being my anchor. That's not to say we couldn't talk about the illness, we did, a lot. In the last few months when she stopped writing and became very depressed, we talked and talked, and that was the toughest time for me. Because what do you say to someone literally weeks away from dying, 'Cheer up, it could be worse', or 'Come on, why the long face? You never know, it might never happen'? But, of course, it was going to happen and it did.

Weeze had a great ability to learn and it only took her a couple of hours with Gav to work out how to load her own entries on to the website and then, that was it, she was off. She sent her soul out into the ether and captured a world.

1 February

    Big girls, they don't cry-y-y (they don't cry)
    Big girls, they don't cry.

If one more person tells me categorically that I'm not going to die I shall punch them. Now, I'm aware that this is probably misdirected anger and that I should be angry with the cancer, if anything, but honestly, it makes me want to scream. So –

a friend of a friend of yours had cancer and they were written off by doctors and then they saw a homeopath and it just disappeared. Well, that's just fabulous. A friend of a friend of mine won the lottery. But I don't tell people who are in debt that a rational answer to their problems is to spend all their time buying lottery tickets. Yes, it may just go away. But the odds are that it won't. And I'm damned if, having been given this warning, I'm going to die unprepared. I figure if I do a load of practical preparations over the next couple of months, then I can relax and live however long I've got left TO THE FULL. So. A recipe book for Tim. A few letters for Caitlin – 'For When You Miss Me', 'For When You Get Married', 'For When You're 27, Like Me' – that kind of thing. 'Dear Caitlin, please disregard all the times I read you Cinderella. Be nice to your stepmother.' Weird. The usual wills and money stuff – 'Please assist me (wink, wink) should I go bonkers when it enters my brain.' Then once my 'affairs are in order' I can get on with the all-important tasks I have set myself:

To cuddle Caitlin as much as is humanly possible – how many memories do I have from when I was three?

To do as much photography as possible – TO MAKE MY MARK.

To try to make Tim as happy as he makes me.

Sometimes it's so awful that I can't bear to think at all. But sometimes it really is like the Travolta film, *Phenomenon* – life has such a wonderful intensity that I feel as though it is a gift, not a disease.

And with that simple entry she started a remarkable document. The last sentence was to become a theme of Weeze's illness. She was very split between the higher state of reality she gained from facing death and the hard evidence of the price she'd have to pay for it. I remember walking around our local shopping centre, a hideous cathedral of consumerism. I had just been thinking how appalling the place was, how it sucked the life out of people, sending them into a shopping coma, when Weeze grabbed my arm and kissed me.

'This orange juice, is unbelievable.' She sipped again at the drink I had just bought her from M&S. Her face was lit up. 'I can't tell you what it tastes like, it's just so – mmmm. Everything is so fabulous. Kiss me.'

She could find beauty in everything in life. I would occasionally find her crying and when I'd put my arm round her she'd just look up at me and say something like 'It's all so wonderful.' I'm not sure how usual this kind of response to a terminal illness is. Although I was grateful for this for her, for me it just made the divide between us seem all the more wide. Dying is a lonely business, not just for the one dying but for those that love them. Because each person has to face the journey in their own way. I got none of Weeze's optimism or *joie de vivre*. For me it was all bleak and dark and impenetrable. All I got out of the experience was the pain of watching and waiting.

5 February

I'm so tired. Yesterday I felt so tired that for a split second I thought of death in terms of rest. I doubt I'll win any positive thinking points for that one. I got pretty down on Wednesday and thought – oh, here it comes, this is how you're supposed to feel about dying, I must have been in denial up to now –

but then it turned out that it was just PMS. I feel much happier now. Mind you, it doesn't seem strictly fair that I should have terminal cancer and PMS.

A couple of times last week people have been over for dinner and the conversation has turned to how cynical the world is now, or how terrible politicians are, or how we're destroying the earth, and I've felt really detached and almost bored – as though I can't muster any strong emotion about it, because it's not really my problem any more. I suppose I could be concerned about the world for Caitlin, but what will be will be, whether I sit and worry about it or not. I suppose that's the case with everything really – and that's why I'm not too depressed by this dying thing; I'll either die or I won't (well, in the near future), but whatever happens I will cope in some way, because that's what happens – people get ill and die all the time and life still goes on for everybody else. I don't see that it's such a huge thing, really; everyone dies and just because we as a society can't deal with it or even talk about it, doesn't make it any less natural.

I spent most of today waiting for a phone call from a doctor in Sheffield who has something called a gamma knife. So far he's the only person who has shown any signs of wanting to talk to me about treating me – but he didn't ring. He's got all my scans and treatment history, but he's going to Australia next week for a month. I really hate waiting for news. In a way I'd rather he rang and said he couldn't treat me than just didn't ring.

Song for the day: 'Who Wants To Live Forever?' By Queen.

Waiting for results or phone calls was the hardest thing over the years of her illness. When she was first diagnosed we had the agony of waiting to see if anyone could do

anything. After the operation we had the anxiety of waiting for the re-scan results. Then every three months we would have to travel up to Guy's Hospital in London where Prof Gleeson would examine her and give us the all-clear or not. These regular check-ups were the worst. Weeze and I would both know we were getting close to one because we'd start getting nervous and we'd stop talking about her cancer. As if, if we talked about it, it might be there next time the Prof looked up Louise's nose.

During her remission we must have been up to Guy's twelve or so times, and it never got any better. In fact, the further away we got from the operation and the further we were into her remission, the more frightening the trips got. Partly because we knew that they'd been unable to remove all of the cancer and so it was only a matter of time before it came back and also because the longer it went on the more we got back to a normal life and the more precious that became. Enjoying watching Caitlin grow up, Weeze's amazing flourishing of her photographic talent, me getting on with writing and directing – life was good and neither of us wanted that taken away. I personally got very jumpy and hyper before the meetings, wanting to bounce around like a rubber ball, but Weeze would get very calm. This was always the way with us in times of stress, I got loud and over-excited and Louise turned into some kind of Zen master.

My bowels were the thing that always took the full brunt of my nerves. I have suffered from IBS ever since this thing started. I remember one time with absolute horror. We were waiting in the hideously depressing old waiting-room to get our results from the Prof. We'd timed it badly again, as we always did. The Prof is a marvellous man who takes his time with his patients, which when you're in with him makes you feel like you're the most special patient in the world and that he's there just for you. However, when you've been waiting for three hours, because each appointment is five minutes long but he takes half an hour with each, it is difficult to keep your nerves in check.

'I'm just popping to the loo, won't be a sec.'

Weeze nodded sagely at me and got back to her *Cosmo*.

Now, the toilets at Guy's are somewhat less than pleasant and as I pulled down my trousers to evacuate my bowels – by the way, skip forward a bit if you're of a nervous disposition, this does little to further our story, it just made me and Weeze laugh. Well, Weeze laugh really. Anyway, I looked down at the toilet seat and somehow couldn't bring myself to sit on it. I'm a hypochondriac on a minor level, and looking down at that seat and knowing all the potentially disease-ridden people that had sat on it, I just couldn't bring myself to. But I knew that I only had seconds to go before I exploded. So I decided to perch somewhat precariously above the seat. What I hadn't expected was the force with which my nerves would project my bowel movement. I swear there was a bang as it left me. I turned round and there it was, all over the seat, the cistern, the back wall of the toilet. As if I wasn't feeling bad enough, this had to happen. I spent twenty minutes in there cleaning it all up. I nearly threw up a couple of times. The only good thing was it took my mind off the meeting, but that was small recompense. When I eventually emerged, I was weak and pale, and Weeze asked me what had happened. When I told her in my best pathetic voice, expecting a hug and some sympathy, she howled with laughter, and the more I tried to explain the horror of it to her, the more she laughed. So when we eventually went in, both of us were giggling like kids and

Prof Gleeson said, 'Nice to see you two in such fine form.'

That was a bit of a pattern in our relationship. I'd make a fool of myself, she'd laugh, then I'd laugh, then we'd keep laughing until we'd forgotten what we were laughing about. Damn, I miss that.

6 February

I'm floundering somewhat. It's like: 'Ladies and gentlemen, your world is about to end. In the meantime do not panic as normal service will continue. Kindly go about your daily grind and restrict your "freaking out" to designated times and places. Do not request more information, as none is currently available. We thank you for your attention and have a nice day.'

I was cooking dinner this evening and desperately wanted to just leave and walk away from everything. As though if I don't see another doctor ever again I can't die, or as though if I don't have to die in front of Tim and Caitlin it won't hurt us.

For days I've been wanting a rest from the constant stream of visitors and going out to dinner, but tonight it felt so strange to be in. I kept hearing clocks ticking. All I could think of was that I really ought to do some ironing, but it just seemed so ridiculous to even consider spending one of my precious evenings ironing that I . . . watched nothing in particular on TV, too tired to get up and go to bed. But here I am now, in bed 11.16 p.m., feeling as though writing this is the most constructive thing I've done today. At least here I'm attempting to unravel my feelings and make sense of – well, at least some part of it all.

Maybe Glen Hoddle and his ilk are right and I did something

ghastly in my last life or my soul chose to have cancer in this life to learn some vital lesson that will help me grow as a whole, or maybe there is no reason and it's just how it is. Or even if there is a reason, we don't/can't know it, so it doesn't matter. Probably I should just learn to be with whatever this throws up and enjoy the rollercoaster (man).

Well, that's worked off some of today's angst. Over and out.

When Louise got ill first time someone told us about Deepak Chopra, a New Age guru who believes that we can heal ourselves. No sooner had we been told about him than we found out he was speaking in Kensington. This we thought was obviously fate, it was too much of a coincidence – maybe this man would show us the way forward. We sat there and listened to him talking for two hours. He sure is some speaker – no notes, charisma coming out of him like a steam train, washing over the audience of devotees – and every single word he said drove Weeze and me crazy. It is entirely possible that we were what our New Age friends would call 'unreceptive' and possibly we were 'blocking', but the message that came over loud and clear made us furious. If you love yourself and those around you enough, you will live. And you cause your own illness. Now, let's get this straight right up front. This is rubbish, shit, and it's evil. Louise didn't hate herself, didn't have any deep-seated self-loathing, wasn't abused as a child. She just got ill, her body just did it itself. All this kind of thinking does is set up a pattern of guilt and accusation. People have got to realize that people die, sometimes they die young, and sometimes no matter how sorted and spiritually in tune they are with the universe they still die. We all die. Frightening, isn't it? More of this as we go on, but I thought I'd just put in my first firing shot across the bows of this kind of stupidity.

7 February

Today was a far, far better day. Possibly because it was sunny. When I stare into a blue sky I can feel myself lifting – it's the best drug – especially after it's been dark and gloomy for a while. Also a nice walk with Tim and Caitlin and then some photography work – press pictures for *The Cherry Orchard* – where I felt in control and comfortable. Got offered three more jobs – one of which I turned down – but great – people really seem to think I'm a good photographer now. Typical. I finally discover something I adore doing and am good at and then I have to go and die. If I really want it enough, will that keep me alive?

9 February

Yesterday Prof Gleeson called to say that 'The Doctor' in Sheffield had looked at my scans and decided that he couldn't do anything. It felt really odd. This guy had told Gleeson that he would definitely talk to me and was really sure he could help. Then he looked at the pictures of the tumour and realized he couldn't. I feel like it is definite now, confirmed. There is nothing that can be done. And I just don't believe in alternative medicine. I am taking the vitamins recommended by the Bristol centre to keep me as healthy as possible and to help me deal with the extra stress, but I don't expect them to cure me. I shall live or die as fate decrees.

Yesterday Tim bought me a book of love poetry and I cried a little whilst reading it. We haven't had enough time together yet – seeing old couples makes me sad.

I spoke to the hospice today for the first time in two and a half years. A counsellor is coming over to talk to me and Tim on Thursday – mainly to talk about Caitlin. He was very nice on the phone and said I was being a really good mother by thinking about it now – apparently a lot of people can't bear to think about dying until the last minute when they then blurt it out to their family and it is more traumatic than it could have been.

Last night I was convinced I could feel it, growing inside my head. I'm sure I can't really – I don't think there are many nerves there. I think I was just imagining it.

This morning I woke up and it was snowing. I got to see Caitlin's face when she looked out of the window and then dragged me out of the house to play in it. Each day of my life is worth a year of a life with no one to love. It is 5.30 now and I'm looking out of the window and it's so quiet. I think the sky is the most beautiful thing; it's the thing that can always lift me out of myself, no matter where or what. When I die I want to be looking out of the window.

Snow is a beautiful thing, which wraps the world up and makes everything look new and fresh and different. We both loved it. Before Caitlin came along, when we could still just leave the house in the middle of the night and go for long walks, one of our favourite things was walking late night in the snow. I remember taking Weeze out for a Valentine's meal the year after we got married and while we were in the restaurant a really heavy snow hit Tunbridge Wells. We were lucky to get the car home. We sat on our balcony, all wrapped up with hot chocolate in our hands, and watched it silently cover the town. It was perfect.

At about two o'clock in the morning we decided to walk round the town. The whole place was deserted, pavements and roads were indivisible under the whiteness. The parks became featureless and muffled. The whole experience was ours and ours alone. We didn't see one other person, not one car, and for those couple of hours we owned the whole town. It was a magic Winterland. We held gloved hands and then, needing the touch of skin, faced the cold and took them off to hold each other without any interference from cloth. We kissed, we laughed, we ran along the roads having sliding competitions to see who could slide the furthest. Weeze always won, because she had little regard for her own safety, and she would hurtle along the road before planting her feet and skidding yards. More often than not she'd go flying over on to her bum, but she didn't mind that – that's the advantage of snow, it cushions the blow.

We had done a huge circuit of the town and were just about to turn into our road when we met our only fellow traveller that night. A beautiful deep red fox poked its head out of a hedge not more than ten feet in front of us. Neither of us spoke, worried we'd spook it, we just followed it in silence up the road as it darted from one side to the other looking for something – food I suppose, but it felt very like a scene from *Alice In Wonderland* or one of the Narnia books. It could have been looking for treasure or a magic key, its curiosity and considered nature making it look quizzical, very human. It headed in and out of people's gardens and finally, just a few feet away from our house, it turned, looked at us and lifted its head, sniffing the air. It then lolloped away across the park next to our house, disappearing into the night. Still without talking, we made our way to bed and made love until the dawn light crept in through the window and we slept.

14 February

So. We were going to be in New York now. Valentine's Weekend with the coolest reservations in the coolest restaurants, tickets for the *Late Show*, Woody Allen's jazz club, backstage tours of Broadway musicals ... it really couldn't have been more exciting. And instead a morning at Heathrow hearing about striking pilots of American Airlines. We were offered a flight that left 'at least' eight hours later and no guarantee of getting home on time. Squandered half of our re-converted dollars on a really marvellous meal at the Criterion – foie gras and Dom Perignon. Then wandered around miserably for hours before returning home, flatter than the proverbial pancake.

I really can't believe our luck. I mean, what the hell am I doing wrong?

This was a big blow. I am notoriously frightened of flying and travel, ever since our honeymoon, and it took all my strength to face this trip. It was one of the things that Weeze really wanted to do, one of the things she wanted to tick off before dying, and because of a stupid airline fuck-up it was screwed up. I think it was the disappointment and the anti-climax which led to my minor meltdown that night. As we walked round London at night the enormity of what we were facing slowly dawned on me. We walked down through Whitehall and down to the river, just chatting about it all, about how strange life was and how sad it was, and then I was crying, crying and crying, and Weeze was cradling me in her arms, the smell of her soothing me. She stroked my hair and kept telling me it would be all right.

'Who knows, maybe I won't die. Although I've got to be honest, it doesn't look that great, does it?'

I wanted her to promise me she wouldn't die. Stupid, I know, but I felt like if she would just say it, just swear to me that she wouldn't die, then she wouldn't. But, ever the grown-up, she looked at me and said, 'I can't promise that, my sweet, I just can't, but I promise you, you'll be OK whatever happens. You won't collapse, you won't have another breakdown, you'll be fine. You have to be for Caitlin. It'll be OK.'

That was enough to calm me, as it always was, whatever happened to us, however I felt. Weeze would just tell me it was OK and I'd believe her. Talk about a mug. But it's these words that are keeping me going now, after she's gone. I can hear her telling me I'll be OK. I pray she's telling the truth.

21 February

Yesterday was my little sister's birthday. She won't speak to me unless I apologize to her husband for asking her if he hit her. Bearing in mind the fact that she had bruises on her face and her husband refuses to meet any of our family, I figured it was a legitimate question and can't quite bring myself to apologize. I have asked her to make peace with me because I am ill and she said my illness wasn't relevant and she wasn't interested. I worry that if I die she'll feel bad for the next sixty years because she wouldn't speak to me, but I don't really miss her in my life. It's strange because when we were young we were really close.

25 February

I read something that helped me to feel all right about my sister. It was in an interview with Oprah Winfrey, of all people. She said that for years she had thought forgiving people meant 'embracing them and inviting them to dinner', which she just couldn't bring herself to do. Then she was told it meant to let go of any hope that the past could be different. I think that's the key with my sister. Forgiving her just means letting go of the hope that she will change.

I have recently read something else – this time something that made me really, really angry. Someone sent me a book called *Mind Over Cancer* by Colin Ryder Richardson. The person who sent it to me is very nice and wanted to help, and hadn't actually read it, but anyway, here are two choice quotes:

'Young children with cancer are only young persons with stresses similar to adults. Here one should look towards the parents for the cause of the cancer. Has the child been rejected or fought over by the parents? Is the home or school environment bad? Is the child bullied or torn emotionally in some other way? A husband or wife may be locked in an endless war at each other's throats. They are the cause but the child suffers by being unable to live a healthy life in such an acidly cancerous place even though it is called home.'

'Perhaps you are young and have breast cancer – so why have you got this illness? Have you been on the pill? Have you had affairs of the heart too often? If you are a mother, have you naturally breastfed children? Has your past life been totally blameless? Haven't you somehow abused yourself sexually? Most cancers are preventable and are found mainly in persons guilty of self-abuse.'

Can you believe it? Can you imagine having a child with leukaemia and being told it's your fault? Or being told you've got cancer because you didn't/couldn't breastfeed your children? Amongst my friends I know that those who have problems breastfeeding feel guilty enough as it is, without this kind of judgemental crap being bandied about. It is true that the author tells people not to feel guilty for past mistakes, but then writes things which seem specifically designed to inspire guilt.

A word of advice here for anyone who knows anyone with cancer or any other illness – really think about the stuff you give them. Read any books or leaflets you give them. Take time to think about how they will receive them. It is far better to just not give them anything than feel like you have to help and give them the wrong thing. I know from time to time Weeze did look at her life and tried to see if there was something in there that could have given her cancer, something she'd done, or hadn't done, even though she was a totally rational good human being. I hate all those who put this crap out for just this reason – I wouldn't have had her feel bad about herself for one second.

To be fair to Mr Ryder Richardson, I understand that all his writings come from the fact that he believes he cured himself of cancer and that he believes he has a responsibility to pass on the valuable insights he's gained.

And that's fine and so here I feel it is important for me to tell the world the insights I've gained. All these people who produce such nonsense are either liars, fraudsters or severely delusional. That's what I honestly believe and I think it's empowering for people with an illness to face up to this possibility. If you can't and you need the support that you can get from these people, then that's great. You must do whatever you can do to feel good about yourself and feel as positive for as long as you can. But whatever you do, don't beat yourself up, don't examine your life looking to apportion blame. No good can come from that. The past is the past – if you've only got a limited time, then live it, and that goes for everyone.

26 February

My mother was talking to me about God the other day, saying that if I believed in God it would make me less afraid of dying. But I'm not really afraid of dying – it's all the stuff beforehand I'm worried about. Besides, I find the idea of a secular sleep a lot less scary than judgement.

Chapter 3

———

10 March

A strange week. Since I last wrote a lot has happened. A meeting with my surgeon went well – we talked about cameras, cancer and God – you know, the usual stuff.

There is a guy at Bart's Hospital who has agreed to talk to me about radiotherapy treatment, so Tim and I are going up to London on Friday to talk to him.

Meanwhile I've started getting a few symptoms, which has knocked me a bit. I get a sharp stabbing pain in my head and some balance problems. The most disheartening thing is my loss of taste, as chocolate and champagne have been my main sources of consolation for the last couple of months. Still, maybe I'll lose some weight, as food is far less interesting to me at the moment.

It's far easier to be flippant about dying when you don't

feel ill. Since the weekend I've been a little down. I think I had thought I would have no symptoms for a little longer, and don't really feel ready to start getting ill yet. So, I thought I would get some of the practical details done quickly and I re-wrote my will yesterday. Slightly more freaky is what I'm doing tomorrow: visiting our local crematorium/cemetery to check out what kind of funeral I want and possibly even to book it or pay for it or whatever you do. It's something I want to do so that Tim doesn't ever have to sort out the details. I thought I'd do it now because if I wait much longer I think I might lose my nerve. I'm going with a friend, as I think going with Tim might be too heavy.

12 March

Yesterday I booked my plot at the cemetery. Very strange, but I got quite excited. Not like buying a house or anything, but still, location, location, location. The old stone chapel is very picturesque, if a little small, and the plot I've chosen is great – between a huge tree and a bench, so Tim and Caitlin can sit and talk to me. The guy said for an extra £60 I could have it dug deep enough for two, which sounded reasonable so I went for that, which I think freaked Tim out a little. I've decided on a burial instead of a cremation. I've been to both and I always think cremations are a little like registry office weddings – ugly buildings, no sense of occasion and another load of people queuing up to go in as soon as you leave. Also, on a more serious note, I think seeing a coffin being lowered into the ground is so final that it is easier to let go and grieve. When I was six my grandmother died and I had a dream about her being burnt in our sitting-room fireplace that was so vivid I can remember it now.

I'm currently on a train going up to Bart's Hospital to talk to the radiologist there. I have no idea what he thinks he can do for me, but I'm trying not to get too excited. My mood is a little suspicious, though, too ebullient for my liking, so if this meeting isn't any good, I fear the next entry may be somewhat miserable. I came out of the house this morning singing 'We're off to see the wizard, the wonderful wizard of Oz', so goodness knows what my subconscious is expecting today. Oh well, Tim wants a go on the computer to play 'Snood', so I'll sign off. Pip, pip.

Unfortunately, or perhaps fortunately for my lawyer and publishers, I can't remember the doctor's name that we saw at Bart's that day. If I could, I'd plaster it all over here in big letters, give you all his address and phone number and warn the world about him. But as it is, I haven't got the foggiest idea what it was.

We got a taxi from the station and held hands all the way. However much you try not to get excited about these things, you always do. In the face of death you find yourself grabbing desperately at anything which might help. There's also a large area of denial – as you walk through the doors of the hospital with your wife, you just know that someone somewhere will be able to help. They have to be able to. The person you know, love, hold, kiss, can't just die on you, someone has to be able to do something. But sometimes nobody can do anything. There was some kind of record sale in the foyer of the hospital and I flicked through the world music stuff while Weeze found out where we had to go. She came and dragged me away and we were led to a waiting-room. Doctor X was on the phone in his little cubicle.

'I know, I know, it's amazing how many of them come over here and then get ill. You'd think they do it on purpose, they get here, get all the privileges of diplomatic immunity and then they want us to pay for them to be ill, I mean really. Anyway, this one's got a nasty shock coming. Ha ha, yeah, it's terminal. Nothing we can do about it. Look, gotta go, yeah, yeah, sure, see ya Saturday.'

More laughter and then the conversation was over. A middle-aged greying man in a white coat appeared from the door and beckoned us in. I don't know why, it may be my own prejudices, but I took an instant dislike to him. It could have had something to do with his last conversation, but it was more than that, something to do with demeanour. He was what I'd call an old-fashioned doctor, not a doctor who believed he worked in partnership with the patients but who believed that he was the boss and you were lucky to be seeing him and he'd do whatever he thought was best for you. Worst of all for me, he had no knowledge of Weeze's case. He asked her a whole host of questions before saying, 'You had radiotherapy before, and at that level, well, you can't have any more. I don't know why you're here to see me.'

He then proceeded to look, for the first time, at her scans. He flicked the large plastic sheets up on to the light box and gave them the quickest of glances, shaking his head all the time. 'No,' he said, in a very matter of fact way, 'it's very bad, multi-site disease, I can't help you.' He then took the scans down, put them back in their envelope and handed them over to Louise.

'You might as well keep these, the NHS will only lose them'.

Then, shell-shocked, we wandered down endless corridors, back out into the light. Weeze looked at me and said, 'Well, I guess that's it then.'

I was destroyed. A lot of people over the year kept saying to us 'You must have hope, hope will keep you going.' The fact is that hope can be incredibly painful, especially when there is no real hope.

Of all the doctors we met during this process, and there were a lot of them, this guy was the only duff one. But, boy, was he an arsehole. And in one ten-minute meeting he nearly tainted all our experiences with the medical profession. Nearly, but not quite. The doctors we got on with the best and still look on as great physicians were the ones who treated us like equals, like intelligent human beings capable of understanding what was going on and capable of making decisions for themselves about what treatment to accept.

Our GP, Clive, and the Prof made that last year and the whole time Weeze had cancer so much easier because they made us feel part of the team looking at her illness. Her opinions were as valid as any other member of the team. She was allowed to weigh up the pros and cons of treatments and procedures. It should also be said that this was largely due to Weeze's attitude herself. She always respected the doctors she had but was never in awe of them, never thought of them as being anything but people with specialized knowledge which could or couldn't help her. A very healthy attitude to have towards your doctors. I was at college with enough medical students to know what they're really like. Let's not put them on a pedestal, they're just people doing a job – it's your body, your illness, don't be pushed or bossed into anything you don't want. That having been said, our guys went over and way above the call of duty for us. They gave up private time, they were always available and they did everything humanly possible to make Weeze comfortable. For that I will always be eternally grateful and will always hold them in my heart. There's not an ounce of me that thinks any more could have been done for Weeze, and if it hadn't been for that idiot at Bart's I'd have had nothing to complain about at all.

14 March

Mothering Sunday

A really great day but tinged, as they say, with sadness. Like, possibly my last Mother's Day, another day on the calendar for Caitlin and Tim to miss me lots, etc., etc., etc. It was a great day, though. Tim's brother, Jay, his wife Lou and their children, Rowan and Holly, came down from London and all of us and Dave, Tim and Jay's father, went to the Ashdown Forest for a picnic. The girls were excited because it is the Hundred Acre wood of Winnie-the-Pooh fame and had a great time because it was so warm and the views are great – so much space, you feel yourself relaxing and breathing more deeply.

15 March

It's a sunny day and I feel fabulous. Have decided that today, for one day only, I don't have cancer. I have been singing and spring cleaning and remembering the countless times I have cleaned this kitchen whilst listening to the Mamas And The Papas or some other such sing-a-long music, back doors open and sun streaming into the house. I could be twenty or sixty and the day-to-day of my life would probably be the same.

However long you live, if you've had a life, it's OK. That doesn't sound like it makes sense, but I mean that I think I've lived long enough to know what life's about.

This was my Weeze! This was how I hope to remember her in the years to come. Not cleaning – because however many times she said she did it, neither of us were brilliantly tidy people – but in the kitchen, dancing. It was our favourite pastime. The hours we spent kitchen dancing must run into weeks. Kitchen dancing for any out there not familiar with it is the kind of dancing you do on your own, only you do it with your loved one in the kitchen with the music playing very loud. You do all the movies you've seen John Travolta in or ballet moves or slow smooching or anything you feel like. I can't recommend it highly enough – it's one of the most life affirming things I can think of.

22 March

Looking back over this diary, I am worried that it might look as though I spend most of my time brooding on dying and feeling irritated by people. It's like when I wrote diaries in my teens – when I am busy and happy I don't think about writing, or I am too busy to write, and then when I look back it looks as though I was miserable for six years, which isn't remotely true.

So in this entry I want to set the record straight. Now is a good time to do it, as I am sitting in Caitlin's room waiting for her walls to dry and feeling fabulous. Tim and I are painting her room while she's at school. It is a really sunny yellow –

like Cornish ice-cream. Painting it feels like slapping custard on the walls. I want to make her room really fun – we're doing handprints of all three of us on the walls next and writing our names and odd happy words around the edges.

Today I spoke to an old school friend whom I haven't seen in years and she couldn't think of anything to say to me. She said, 'Normally I would say look on the bright side, but there isn't a bright side. There just isn't a bright side, is there?'

Well, Amanda, yes there is.

I have a really cool life. I live in a big house next to a park with a playground in it. I have tons of the most supportive friends I can imagine – friends who do so much for me (Jane and Uschi, I'm so lucky I have you) – friends who I know will look out for Tim and Caitlin always. My family is also fabulous – I would trust mine and Tim's parents with Caitlin for ever, and I have two lovely sisters who are great to talk to.

If I died tomorrow I would have still known more love in my life than most people experience in eighty years. I still consider myself a really lucky person. And, weirdly enough given the circumstances, I think a lot of my friends still consider me lucky. To be honest, I would rather be dying than be married to someone else or have a different child. So I can't be unhappy with my lot. If I had the chance to throw away my cards and get a new deal, I'd still play the hand I've got, because highs and lows are better than a healthy life without love or the ability to appreciate the wonder of it all.

Now that's enough schmaltz for now, so I'll sign off.

One last thing, though – if people can't (and they generally can't) think of anything to say to me, I wish they'd say 'supercal-ifrajilisticexpialadocious'. I would laugh my head off if someone said that to me.

And loads of people did say that to her. As soon as that message went up on the website she got loads of guest book messages and emails which said exactly that. And she did laugh. By this time the site was really taking off and she was bowled over that people wanted to read what she had to say. Although she always wanted to write and leave a mark, for a few weeks when she started writing her diary it was very much for her, a cathartic process. But as time went on and more and more people were logging on daily to check on her progress, she began to write for her audience. She felt she had a responsibility to continue it and to be honest about how she was feeling. We had long debates about what the website was for and whether or not she could really be honest on it, and whether or not it was a valuable thing to be doing or mere voyeurism. It was a debate that continued right up until the end of her life and when she got particularly depressed towards the end she sometimes regretted she had ever started it. She looked back on previous entries and felt so different, so somewhere else, that she began to doubt how truthful she'd been earlier on in the diary. But going through it now I know she was honest about how she felt on any particular day, and I am proud of her for it.

24 March

First evening alone for ages. And I can't stop crying . . .

Chapter 4

—

1 April

Tim and I returned from New York the day before yesterday, having had an amazing three days. As our original Valentine's weekend had been cancelled by the airline (strike), we were compensated with first-class upgrades on the flights and a suite at the hotel (overlooking Central Park). Talk about how the other half lives. It was great. We saw a huge Broadway musical, *Ragtime*, went backstage at the *Late Show* (halfway round the world to see Blur!), and saw Woody Allen playing with his jazz band in a club – the highlight of the trip. Tim bought an entire suitcase of clothes and I discovered that my bum is the same size in England as it is in Saks Fifth Avenue, so bought things like stationery and camera stuff – some gorgeous paper from Cartier and playing cards from Tiffany's.

Although I got pretty exhausted and my ear hurt on the

flight, one of the best things for me was that I really felt that I was having a holiday from having cancer. I felt like a tourist having a really romantic weekend, far too busy to think about much at all.

Caitlin had a great time here visiting new-born lambs and things and apparently didn't cry once! So no guilt either! Home to something of an anti-climax, but at least the weather is nice here. Next holiday is France – all together.

One strange thing: flying back from New York I was looking out of the window and saw us flying from sunset to darkness. We were high above the clouds and over the sea and could see nothing but golden orange fading into deep blue, then blackness. I suddenly felt stifled and desperate to turn back into the sun, as though I were dying.

New York was an incredible time for me, I loved it. Yes, it's true, I love New York. Just overcoming my fear of flying to get on a transatlantic flight was quite a big step, but actually getting in the limousine at the other end at JFK and driving across the bridge into Manhattan was a buzz and a half. As Weeze said, as compensation for the last aborted attempt, we'd had nearly everything on the trip upgraded. For those of you who haven't flown business class or first class, it is simply fabulous! Especially, I guess, for a luxury travel virgin like myself. Why? It's the big seats – they're like beds. I swear I felt refreshed when I got to New York, not tired and filthy as if I'd just travelled in a cattle truck, as I normally do. But why the fear of flying?

OK, picture the scene if you will. Weeze and I are on our honeymoon, nearly everything that could go wrong has and we're both sick as parrots. We cut short our cruise down the Nile and decide to fly back to Cairo to just rest up in a nice hotel. Well, on the way from the boat to Luxor airport the taxi breaks down in the middle of the desert. This I should have spotted as a bad omen. The massive fat man driving us turns round and says, 'I don't know what's wrong, you better push.' And he's saying that to a couple who've been throwing up non-stop for ten days, for whom just staying conscious was a difficulty. But being a good English couple, rather than saying 'Sod off, you've got to be joking', we crawled out of the cab and began to push. It was so hot, and such hard work to push this taxi and this huge man that I thought one of us was going to collapse. I had visions of us pushing all day and night and having to drink the fat man's sweat as a method of survival. Luckily, none of this came to pass. Within two minutes another taxi passed us, we hailed it and jumped ship, leaving the fat man to fend for himself. For all I know he's just a skeleton sitting in a taxi in the middle of the desert now.

So we eventually got to Luxor airport only to find that there was no air-conditioned waiting lounge – people just sit round in the heat and get sun stroke – and to be informed that there was no plane for us. Apparently, and I quote, 'The engine fell off your plane in Cairo, so we are without a plane.' Well, call me an old stick-in-the-mud if you like, but I didn't find this terribly reassuring. And I didn't feel a lot better when they told me that there was a plane going up to Cairo that wasn't scheduled to be taking passengers but we could hitch a lift on it if we wanted. Louise had just come back from the toilets for the third time and said she just needed to get out of there, so we headed for the plane. From the outside it looked like a normal plane, but on the inside it was a different story. There was food and litter everywhere and the air hostesses looked at us in horror as we boarded, desperately trying to tidy themselves up, applying make-up and buttoning up blouses.

'I don't like this, this doesn't feel right at all,' I said and, as if to put a further jinx to the whole flight, I added, 'That's exactly what people say on the telly – there's always two people who decided not to get on Death Flight 110 because they had a strange premonition about imminent disaster.'

Weeze shook her head and said, 'It's this plane or the old woman who won't give me enough toilet paper back in the hell hole of a toilet. I'm taking the plane, you do what you like.'

So off we set and everything was going fine for a good twenty minutes. I was looking down for the first time at the beauty of the desert. Images of Peter O'Toole on the back of a camel floated through my mind and then we suddenly dropped five hundred feet out of the air. One second the engines and the wings and all the little flashing lights and knobs had been keeping us airborne, the next minute we were heading for the sand. My stomach, which I'd left some five hundred feet above, took a good few seconds to catch up with me. I turned to Weeze and managed to say, 'Fuck me, that was a bit scary, what . . .' when we hit another series of turbulence pockets, the plane dropped and bounced all over the place and I started to freak out. Singing and laughing as loudly as I could, I tried to remember all the names of the Egyptian gods we'd heard about on our travels. 'Horus, erm . . . Horus, ermm, Amon, Ra, ermm, look any of you, help me and I'll believe, I promise, I'll believe, and I'll make others believe, please oh gods, please help . . .'

Weeze, on the other hand, always became calm in the

face of adversity and with Zen-like peace she whispered to me, 'Tim, we're all frightened, now keep it down a bit.'

At this point the captain came on the tannoy. This was what I wanted, news from the man in charge that things were OK. What I'd hoped for was a very upper-class BA pilot saying, 'I'm terribly sorry, ladies and gentlemen, it's the teensiest bit choppy up here, but we'll soon pass through it and Jeeves will bring round the Earl Grey tea.' But this was not BA and what we got was an Egyptian pilot who sounded more scared than I did: 'It very bad, we try to get out of it.'

At this point the plane went into a severe dive. I could see the dunes getting closer and closer and closer and at what I assumed must be somewhere near the last minute he pulled out of the dive, levelled off and we proceeded on our way more or less without incident. I was so petrified by the experience that when we landed I found myself not only unable to clap and cheer along with the rest of the passengers, but unable to walk. I stood up and found my legs had turned to jelly. Much to Weeze's amusement, I weaved my way down the aisle like a drunk man.

Ever since then, flying has been a somewhat nerve-racking experience. Except in first class on the way to New York. That was a dream and Weeze was stunning all weekend. She was radiant, gorgeous and – most importantly – alive, really alive, glowing, absorbing every experience. We did the whole Big Apple thing, we went up the Empire State Building at night, wandered round Times Square in the rain, went to the Metropolitan Opera House – it was all so New York.

Weeze suffered from jet lag or was just getting more tired, but overall she was on top form. In the mornings she had trouble getting up and there seemed to be no need to push on too early. I, however, got up each morning at five and didn't really know what to do with myself. I would spend half an hour or so watching her sleep. She looked really peaceful, as if she'd left the cancer behind her in England. But the longer I watched her, the longer I felt I was pushing my luck. After a while I would inevitably be hit by a melancholy, as I realized that one day I'd be alone and that she wouldn't be with me, in my bed, sleeping peacefully. At this point I'd put on some shorts and my trainers and head off for a jog round Central Park in the early morning light. It was chilly and frosty and surprisingly empty. It felt like it was my park. And as parks go, that's a pretty good one to have. The cold air was sharp and chilled my lungs as I ran. I loved running round to Strawberry Fields, then out of the park over to Lennon's apartment where he was shot, then down to the Met Opera House, down further to Times Square and then back to the hotel. Normally by the time I'd finished my run it was still only 6.30 so I'd find a café and chill out there, just watching New York life for an hour or so.

When I'd had enough of gawping, I'd make my way back to the hotel and wake Weeze with a kiss and a coffee. We shopped like there was no tomorrow. Or rather, I did, while Weeze bought the odd little thing that would come wrapped in a beautiful paper bag. I bought eight pairs of Levi's, thirty t-shirts, baseball hats, shoes – you name it, I bought it. I don't know why, I usually hate shopping, but New York just had everything I wanted by the bucketload.

A lovely friend of ours, Sally, had more or less organized the whole trip for us. She was so sweet. All our dinner appointments were at the grooviest restaurants and everywhere we went we got VIP treatment – it made us both feel very special. But there are some times when being treated like a VIP is a good thing and other times when it can all backfire. One of the things we were most excited about was the fact that Sally had got us tickets to see Woody Allen play jazz at this little club. So we got all dressed up and headed down to the venue. When we got there we hadn't realized the lengths Sally had gone to. We thought we had to wait with everyone else, pay for our tickets and then squeak in at the back. So we spent half an hour out in the cold with the other people queuing up on the off-chance of picking up a ticket. Getting cold and losing patience, Weeze told me to go and check up front to see if Sally had left us tickets to pick up. So I managed to push my way through to the *maître d'* and apologetically asked if there were tickets for Tim and Louise. This slightly camp guy gushed, 'You're here, at last you're here. Fabulous, where's Louise? Come on, quickly bring her in. Quickly, the show's about to start.'

So we were ushered past all the waiting fans like we were film stars and taken into the room. It was tiny and could have seated no more than a hundred people, all of whom were already seated and drinking at their tables. Much to our disbelief we were led to the front table. It was no more than two feet away from the small dais where the band would be playing. Champagne and glasses were rushed to the table by numerous waiters and everyone in the whole place looked at us as if wondering who we were. Then in came Woody and the band. And there he was, sitting right in front of us, literally within an arm's length, one of the century's greatest filmmakers.

In fact, he was so close it was almost embarrassing – wherever you looked, there he was, exactly like in his movies, nervy and twitchy, fiddling with his clarinet's reeds, looking nervous and uncomfortable, ill at ease with the world. Then he was playing and his clarinet sang. His furrowed brow relaxed and he entered his own world, oblivious to the packed room in front of him. Oblivious to the hundreds of flashes from the cameras that everyone seemed to have smuggled into the club. So many, in fact, that I kept checking Weeze, worried that they'd have some kind of strobe effect and send her into a fit.

I'm no jazz expert, as my good friend and ex-jazz editor for *Time Out* Linton will tell you (I thought Duke Ellington was eighth in line to the throne), but he sounded wonderful – quite raw, quite unschooled, but the music was coming from somewhere deep inside him and as such was transfixing. Each player in the band took their turn to show off their own musical virtuosity and after each break the crowd applauded and cheered their appreciation. Midway through the gig Woody took a middle eight and swung out some angel licks which made me laugh with joy. As he finished, the crowd stayed quiet and one solitary English voice could be heard to shout out, 'Nice one, Wood!' Why the crowd chose that moment not to cheer, and why I chose those very words, so very loudly, is a mystery. Why I couldn't have said 'Woody' or 'Woody Allen' or even 'Mr Allen' – anything would have been better than the over familiar 'Wood'. A flush of horror came over me. Louise, ever the supportive wife, turned her head away from me and pretended for the next half hour that she wasn't with me but was with the big fat Mafia boss to our left who was fondling a very young Russian girl. Yes, she'd rather have pretended to be a mobster's hooker than be with the geeky English guy who shouted out 'Nice one, Wood!' at the top of his voice.

Outside she laughed about it, then got in a cab with the old guy and the Russian princess and headed off up

42nd Street. She got back to the hotel at about five in the morning, stinking of pasta and cheap caviar, and had a large roll of notes tucked into her bra. OK, the last bit isn't true but I was just seeing if you were paying attention. It wasn't really that large.

When I look back on New York I look at it as being the big trip, the big gesture. It was luxurious, extravagant and joyful. I can still see Weeze's face as she first opened the door to the suite we had in the hotel and walked from room to room. 'Tim, look, there's another room, and look at the view, wow, we're right on top of Central Park.' We drank champagne in bed and made love late into the night – it was three of the best days of my life. But, as with all good things, it had to come to an end and as we flew home both of us felt the slight sick feeling of knowing we were flying back to our real life, flying back to the cancer. The image she talked about while looking out of the plane window became a very strong one for her and she often found herself dreaming of being dead and floating on clouds in a strange golden sunset light. She found it very peaceful, she felt released – no longer held to the ground by the pain of a mortal body, she was soaring, pure spirit, pure joy.

3 April

The world is a strange place; one day it is so sunny and I can think of a million things to miss and to prove what a wonderful place this is and the very next day the sky is a blank wall of grey and everyone seems to be talking about war. Now even more than ever before I just cannot understand war. And at the moment I don't want to think about it. The news just upsets me without making me feel more in touch with the world.

Next week off to France. Keep on running!

4 April

I'm watching *The Big Chill* and feeling nostalgic. Although for what, I'm not sure. The last time I watched it I was much younger and I assumed that I had years and years of . . . I don't know. Everything. Of doing things, of being idealistic and then growing cynical and disillusioned and doing more stuff and discovering inner wisdom and . . . you know, all the stuff they do in movies.

Films give us such extraordinary expectations. There is the expectation of extraordinary lives or that we can draw wisdom from our ordinary lives or that they will have a plot. There is a part of me that feels that if my life is really rounding to a close, all those loose ends should be tied up neatly; I want to know what happens in the end to everyone I've ever known.

Emails to the afterlife please.

It's funny reading this one because, of all the people I know, Weeze's life was the one most like a movie. She truly lived an extraordinary life. OK, so it was a tragedy in the end, an ending that leaves the audience in tears and feeling drained, but happier for having had the experience. It's also interesting because I think for a lot of the year it felt like it was a film for us, we felt like the whole thing was unreal – it was so intense that it couldn't possibly be real. I can remember how much of a fraud I felt when I told people about Weeze's illness.

'Yeah, have you heard about Louise?' Pause, meaningful look, slight sadness behind the eyes. 'The cancer's back. There's nothing they can do this time.' Another pause for effect to let the audience fully appreciate the dramatic moment. 'They say she's got a year, possibly two at the most.' More sad looks, possibly think about squeezing out a tear.

It all just sounded so over-dramatic. I couldn't take it in. Well, that's not true, sometimes it crashed in on me and I just couldn't stop crying and then breaking the news to someone was soul-destroying. However, a lot of the time I'd be having a good day, bumbling around the way you do, and then I'd bump into someone and they'd ask how I was and I'd have to make the decision in my head – do I just say fine and keep on moving or do I tell them that I'm facing losing everything and that things couldn't really be any worse? Both Weeze and I found this a real dilemma, because people's reactions were often overwhelming and we didn't want to put people through it. And we could never tell how any particular person was going to react. Some of the strongest people we know just burst into tears, while others who we thought would have been unable to handle it were fabulous and very matter of fact in their sympathy. For some reason, I always found telling people over the phone the hardest thing to do. Still do. I don't know why, but I have trouble saying Weeze has gone on the phone without blubbing my eyes out. Often I can tell people face to face without it really affecting me. Answers from any psychologists on a postcard please.

Well, the Cathar castles are spectacular, the food is by and large delicious, and we spent last night in the loveliest hotel I've ever seen, but it feels artificial being here. Caitlin is having a great time and is really enthusiastic about everything, and I should be able to think of this as an ordinary family holiday to France in the Easter holidays, but somehow I can't. I feel as though I ought to be absorbing every experience more, as though these holiday memories for Caitlin and Tim are super-loaded with significance. As a result, I don't feel terribly relaxed. I am exhausted and dizzy. But the food is fabulous. And so cheap! And Caitlin is a joy to travel with. She is so adaptable and enthusiastic about everything.

Wow, what an amazingly succinct entry. The French trip was a cock-up, but for a few beautiful high points. We got the train over to Paris and picked up a large people carrier. We drove down south in a couple of big chunks and late on the second night we turned up at this house in the middle of nowhere, deep in the Pyrénées. My dad, who came with us on the trip, had arranged to borrow this place that he'd been to before one summer. But when we got there it was somewhat more remote than we had imagined and it was cold and wet and full of spiders. Weeze walked round the house like a haunted woman trying to find one room she could feel comfortable in to settle down, but found no solace. Bless her, she was great at a lot of things, but slumming it wasn't one of them. My dad kept us smiling and said he'd sort it all out, get a fire going, and we'd all be toasty before we knew it. But neither Weeze nor I could see ourselves staying there for two weeks. In fact, we couldn't see ourselves staying there for two nights. We climbed into our tiny double bed, with wet damp sheets and a musty smell, and Weeze broke down. She cried and cried. It wasn't just about where we were, it was about everything, but the place certainly didn't help. Within about two minutes we'd made up our minds that we weren't going to stay any longer than that night and this seemed to cheer Weeze up a bit, and made me incredibly relieved as well.

We shut our eyes for what seemed like seconds before Caitlin, lying between us, woke up crying, and not just crying, but screaming, rolling around the bed holding her tummy. Lights on, action stations. I spent an hour cradling her in my arms, carrying her around, giving her Calpol, singing to her, dancing round with her, anything to make her feel better, but nothing worked. I could take Louise being in pain, I knew we were in it together, but I can't bear it when Caitlin's in pain, I go berserk. I have to keep really calm and just hold her and hold her. After an hour I'd had enough and decided we had to get her to a hospital. It was only then that I realized quite how stupid this choice of holiday home had been. We started our drive at one o'clock in the morning, at three-thirty we made it out of the mountains, at four o'clock we got to the first town. We followed the signs for the hospital, only to be told when we got there that this was a hospital for the insane. Well, we think that's what the guy on the door was trying to tell us with his strange goggly eye motions and tapping of his head. He told us where the nearest proper hospital was and an hour later we were there. Caitlin had been screaming for the best part of five hours, Weeze was distraught, I was in hyper-calm Dad mode and my father was trying his best to keep things light in the car. It turned out she was severely constipated, she was given a rectal examination, and everything was sorted out.

Sitting in the waiting room in Carcassonne, I was suddenly overwhelmed with sadness and a feeling of stupidity. OK, Caitlin was all right, but what on earth would we have done if Louise had been taken ill, if something had popped in her head and she'd needed immediate help? I determined that that was it. I just wanted to get my family home as quickly as possible. We stayed in the house one night longer and then started our journey home. We took it nice and slowly, staying in lovely hotels, eating in only the best restaurants and going to see all the castles and beauty spots we wanted to. But it felt good to be heading home. This was a holiday too far and we would never again go away. We popped into Disneyland Paris for Caitlin, and had a miserable and boring time standing in queues for hours, and wondering to ourselves why on earth we were there. Especially because we'd gone there two years before and had an equally miserable time. So we stayed there all of three hours and then headed into Paris, the most wonderful city in the world.

13 April

I am writing this from the best hotel I've ever been in, or imagined. It is the hotel, in Paris, that Oscar Wilde died in. Of course, it has been done up somewhat, as he died in poverty, and is now the most amazing four-star place. It is the only place I have ever stayed in that combines luxury (I have just been drinking champagne in a lovely old marble bath) with feeling like you're staying in someone's house. The someone, mind you, being a good deal richer than anyone you actually know. My state of relaxation tonight has, I think, to do with the fact that Caitlin fell asleep an hour ago, so I have a chance to catch up with myself, to think selfishly, to write this. I am used to having a bit of time to myself each day, so this week of keeping the same hours as Caitlin and letting her catch up in the car has been emotionally, as well as physically, exhausting for me.

Home tomorrow, I think, back to life, back to reality. And the space to be miserable if I feel like it, and to talk to Tim without having to couch it in terms that Caitlin won't understand.

15 April

Home. It's strange, but I got kind of lured into thinking I was better. Today I was talking to a friend about my whole situation and I got really sad. Tim was there and he said he felt the same way afterwards: as though the crisis had passed and now it's back. Perhaps the family holiday thing did work. Or perhaps one simply can't sustain the intense 'Oh-my-God, I'm dying' feeling forever and now and again you simply forget about it.

16 April

A very ordinary mum kind of day with Caitlin. Tim up in London lunching with his friend Linton, talking about film scripts. Caitlin and I spent the day playing with each other and with my friend Uschi and her son Pete. Caitlin and I were playing doctors and she was pretending to remove her doll

Madeline's appendix and then we had the following conversation:

Me: 'Who do you know who's ill and gets dizzy and has nosebleeds?'
C: 'You.'
Me: 'Do you know why?'
C: 'Your head. What is it?'
Me: 'There's a bit of my head that's growing in the wrong direction and it's pressing on things which makes me dizzy.'
C: 'Oh.'

She then carried on playing, but a bit later she did an operation on a clown's head to 'take out the bit going in the wrong direction'. I told her my doctor in London had wanted to do that, but couldn't. When she asked why not I said it was too tricky. She seemed to accept this, although the clown got fixed up because 'I have tweezers' (from her plastic doctor's kit)!

I felt really good after the conversation, as though I had broached the subject properly for the first time. I am sure now that she knows something is wrong with me. I am torn between feeling that it will be a relief when she knows – for me, in that I won't need to hide my feelings at all – and a desire to preserve her wonderful, happy, innocent world for as long as possible.

I love her so much.

Of all the multitude of things we worried about as a couple over the year, Caitlin was the most common subject of conversation, and one of the only things that always brought both of us to tears. I hated, and still do hate, the idea that this little angel that I live with will grow up not knowing her mother. Lots of people tell me that she'll remember a lot about her, and that through things like the books and the website and all the people who knew and loved her, Caitlin will always remember her and know her. But that's just not true, is it? I know that on some level there's sense in that, but in a very real way Caitlin will never know Weeze. She'll never know the physicality of Weeze, and that's gone for ever. However much I hug her and kiss her, which is far more than an independent-minded little four-year-old would like – 'Dad, get off me, stop kissing me, Dad, I'm trying to watch Dexter's Laboratory' – it's not the same as a hug from your mum. Nothing is. As I was growing up, whenever things were really bad it was my mum that I called for, it was her arms that I wanted to be in, and even in later life when I'm equally as close to my father as I am to my mum, there's still something special about a cuddle with your mum. They're just good at it, fact, and Weeze was really good at it.

There are also all the hundreds of things that come up with kids that you have to make decisions about, tricky stuff, stuff you want to be able to share with someone and check out. I know I've got a good network of friends and family that I can discuss things with, but it's not the same – suddenly it's just me, she's my responsibility and the buck stops with me. Weeze and I would spend hours wandering around doing the 'What Ifs?' game. One I remember was 'OK, so she's fifteen and she wants to go to Glastonbury with her boyfriend who looks like all the wanted posters you've ever seen, what do you do?' My answer ran along the lines of: how would she have a boyfriend at fifteen when I'm going to lock her up in a cupboard from the age of eleven and am only going to let her out when she's reached her mid-forties? If I remember it correctly, Weeze said I should think about it seriously and weigh up how sensible Caitlin is at that particular point in her life, always remembering that trust is a vital thing between parent and child. But just to save time, I'm telling you now, Caitlin, the answer is a big no – now back upstairs and finish that essay or at this rate you'll never get into Oxford or Cambridge.

Then there's a whole host of other stuff I just don't have any clue about. For one thing, there's make-up. During my late teens I experimented quite heavily with make-up but with very little positive effect on my life. Mainly I'd smear lipstick over my lips, so it looked like a nasty gash I got in some fight, and then there was the whole black mascara and eyeliner thing, which made me look like a panda. As you can imagine, these are hardly the best credentials for future tutoring of my child in the mystical ways of the blusher and the foundation. But all that pales into insignificance compared with the terrifying prospect of broaching the whole period thing. Now, it's not that I mind talking about it, that'll be fine – I've read up and I know what's going on – it's the practical side of the whole affair that causes me some kind of anxiety. I'm just not entirely sure how all the different options work. You know, what a heavy or light flow is, what pantyliner you need for whatever situation you're in – I don't know, it's all a nightmare. If it's left up to me, she'll end up looking like Alice Cooper with a tampon up her bum.

20 April

On Saturday night Tim and I were at a party given by some new neighbours, and there were a few people there I didn't know. I had a conversation with one couple about having children; you know, when is the best time and things. I said that Tim and I had Caitlin fairly young – everyone else we know seems to wait until they're thirty these days – and they asked how old I was. Anyway, I heard myself saying, 'I'm glad I had her when I did because by the time she's off at university I'll only be forty-two and can have a whole other career.'

It sounded really strange and echoey coming out of my mouth. It's something I've said countless times before, but it just sounded so false, as though someone else was saying it. I had to gulp down half a glass of wine to stop myself bursting into tears right then.

It has got to the stage now where it is so much a part of my life that it feels strange talking to people who don't know. Our window cleaner gave me a cutting he had saved about a photo competition where the prize is an assignment for the *Independent* newspaper, and he was talking to me all enthusiastically about giving my career a boost. It was so sweet of him that I couldn't tell him I can't go into my darkroom any more without falling over . . .

23 April

Falling over a lot at the moment, and I've discovered that it feels a lot more natural to feel dizzy and fall over when you've had a couple of glasses of champagne. Perhaps I'm beginning to feel ill. Then again, perhaps it's just the sinus infection I'm taking antibiotics for.

I'm having strange dreams at the moment, containing a lot of people I haven't seen or even thought about for years — people from my primary school. I feel like getting in touch with everyone I've ever known — probably an extension of that tying-up-loose-ends thing (see 4 April). The dreams are so vivid, though, that's it's almost as though I'm revisiting the people without having to in real life.

The falling over thing was one of the most dramatic visual signs of Weeze's illness. One minute she'd be talking away quite nicely, the next minute she'd be on the floor. I can remember the heart-stopping nature of the first few times I saw her keel over. It tore my heart out. What was more upsetting was the casual way she took it. 'Well, that was interesting,' she said the first time as I picked her up off the floor. It made everything nerve-racking for me. I could never be certain that when she was out shopping or in charge of Caitlin on her own that she was all right. A couple of times she was out half an hour later than I expected and I got frantic about where she was and what had happened. And this wasn't always without foundation — once she slid to the floor in our local supermarket and another time, while I was working at *Time Out*, I can remember getting a phone call from her at Harrods saying she had fallen and was in the medical centre there being looked after. I went and picked her up and took her home.

The intelligent observer might say, well, why didn't you just stop her from going anywhere on her own? That was eventually what we had to do, but for a fair few months we struggled on, either refusing to accept that this was happening or that we were desperate not to let the cancer change us or the way we lived our life, as if by admitting that it was limiting us we were somehow giving it power. It's also amazing what you can get used to. Before you know it, the fact that your wife keels over two or three times a day and that you have to pick her up and dust her down before starting all over again becomes your norm. The only time you realize it's not normal is when you see the look on other people's faces. Even stuff at the end becomes normal, the full-time care stuff – it's just what you do, it's not horrible or weird or anything. It's just you getting on with the person you love and doing whatever you can to make them as comfortable as possible.

The fact that the falling over affected her photography was a real blow to Weeze. Of everything she did in her life while we were together, the photography was the single most personally fulfilling thing I ever saw her take part in. She was a natural. I remember very clearly the conversation that led to her taking it up. My father had just brought over a beautiful book of Bruce Chatwin's photographs and while Weeze loved them, she kept saying, 'I mean, how hard can that be? If you just take enough shots, you're bound to get some which are fab, aren't you?' I disagreed and said there was a large degree of skill and artistry involved, and so the challenge began. She had a month to come up with five pictures worthy of an exhibition. As soon as she got behind the camera she came alive and, sure enough, the five came easily and by the end of the month she had more than enough to fulfil our criteria. But what had happened was that she wanted to learn more about it, to learn why some shots hadn't worked and why some had when she thought they wouldn't. So she set up a darkroom in our house and started going to evening courses. Her black and white work of Caitlin and our friends was quite exquisite and maybe it was something to do with her cancer, because she was desperate to capture more than just the moment – she wanted to capture a little bit of them, especially when it came to Caitlin. I look at her photos now and can see what she was saying to Caitlin – this is how I saw you, this is the love we shared. It's a choker. She also took the only shot of me that I've ever really liked, which is amazing in itself. It's one of me on the phone, looking very like a writer, and I always said that if I ever got my long-suffering novel published I'd put that on the back. She said I should put it on the back of any book I did for years and years as a good way of attracting women. What a sweety!

25 April

I was talking to some friends last night about ghosts. One of them had a spooky experience and after a bit they got a Catholic priest in to exorcise the house and it worked. Therefore, I think they ought to become Catholic. That is, if they truly believe they saw a ghost and they truly believe the priest's exorcism worked, then they HAVE NO CHOICE but to become a Catholic.

This is kind of how I feel about spiritual healing. I feel that if someone in the name of Jesus Christ 'heals' my cancer, I will have no alternative but to accept Jesus Christ despite my intellectual rebellion against such a thing. I'm thinking about this because some friends of ours wish to introduce me to a Christian healing centre. I'm tempted to go, mainly because it sounds like a nice place to be relaxed and looked after and they have a lot of experience in the field . . . and, of course, never say never.

The last few days I have occasionally caught myself daring

to think that maybe, just maybe, I might get better. The rush of hope I get is awful in that it contains the seed of possible future disappointment. And disappointment of that magnitude is too hard.

26 April

I've been going through my old records – it's amazing the affect music, particularly when it has strong associations, can have on you. Earlier on I was going through loads of old punk singles and I felt more energetic than I have done for weeks. Mind you, at this grand old age I find it very hard to listen to whole tracks of heavier stuff. The Buzzcocks and Clash are still fun to jump around to, but loads of my old records just sound awful in the cold light of adulthood.

Then I played some albums – *Donovan's Greatest Hits* I still know all the words to, despite not having listened to it for about eight years. It's strange how lyrics stay in one's head so long . . . I'm sure that if I go mad and lose my memory at the end I'll still know all the words to 'Wake me up before you go go' (unfortunately).

About half an hour ago I put Pink Floyd on – very rarely a good idea – and started to get morbid . . .

Anyway, I shall sign off now and go and jump around to the Specials.

Strangely enough, she was right – at the end, when everything else was slipping away from her, on the last day she managed to sing all of 'Come On, Eileen' and 'Wombles of Wimbledon', but she'd have been glad that at least there was no Wham. As a teenager, Weeze had impeccable musical taste. When I was running round with a white stripe painted across my face, pretending to be Adam Ant, Louise was collecting rare Jamaican dub records. I remember a dinner where we all sat round and discussed the first records we'd bought and everyone had their embarrassing confessions – mine was 'Grandad' by Clive Dunn – everyone, that is, except Weeze. When she started listing her singles collection it was so cool that hardly any of us had even heard of the people in it – that's how cool she was. And she was cool in that way without thinking about it. She was never conscious of following fashion trends or a cool set, she did what she did and it just happened that everything she was into made her one of those people that you always wanted to be. The sort of person that, when you were with them, you spent most of your time saying to yourself 'Damn, I wish I'd said that.' Or 'Why haven't I read that book?' I always hoped that marrying Weeze made me cool by association. Although I'm not that cool *per se*, the fact that she chose to marry me I always thought was a good sign and that maybe people would look at me and say, 'Geez, he doesn't look much, but if he can woo her he must do something pretty special.'

Chapter 5

———

2 May

The day before yesterday an article about this website came out in my local paper. It is odd how people interpret things. The article was basically meant to be some publicity for the website and that was about it. However, some people read it and decided I was asking the world at large for a cure for cancer. I have therefore had a homeopath phone me, a couple of people drop round books and a leaflet from the Cancer Support Group.

Now this latter was a perfectly reasonable thing to do – in fact the support group would no doubt consider itself negligent if they didn't tell me about what they have to offer. But the trouble with all these treatments is that they are so contradictory. The only thing they seem to have in common is the conviction that they'll work. So some people recommend a strict vegetarian diet – but there is a clinic in South America that claims very good results from a diet of the blood from raw liver. Some recommend a diet very low in fat. And then there's my favourite cure story:

A man had cancer and decided that the cancer was eating him and if he therefore gave it something nicer to eat, it would lay off him. So he drank a pint of double cream a day. He got jolly fat, but he cured himself of cancer. Now most people would think that it is ridiculous to drink cream, but I think it is on a par with the 'frequent coffee enemas' I have been recommended recently.

I think it's down to fate. Some people get better. They then attribute it to whatever they did last, be it cream, coffee, raw vegetable juice or prayer. If I get better I'm going to write a book about how I cured myself of cancer by sticking vanilla pods under my armpit, and see how many copies I sell. Except, of course, I won't because I think it's wrong to sell people coloured water cure-alls and I thought we'd stopped that years ago.

That's enough ranting. And just for the balance, I have been there. I have spent thousands of pounds at various therapists and lived my life entirely around T'ai Chi, meditation and a strict vegetarian diet (for three years). It didn't cure me of cancer, it didn't make me particularly fulfilled and it stopped me enjoying meals out.

The last booklet I was given talks about being either convinced you will get well or despairing. I don't see why one has to be one or the other: I am neither.

The cream story became a kind of mantra for Weeze, something she would repeat over and over again. It was her way of rationalizing her actions. There is a huge pressure placed on those suffering from cancer to take positive action against the illness. I think this is why you often hear things like 'after a brave fight against cancer' or 'her battle against cancer'. Both Weeze and I never felt this, there was no fight, it wasn't something you could rail against, something you could bop on the nose, it was something that she accepted and lived with. But by accepting it she never felt that she was giving in to it, or being fatalistic, she always thought she was just living with it and that it wasn't ruling her life. She was also very conscious of the fact that many people spend the last few years of their lives chasing around the world looking for cures and never find one. And what have they really achieved? They just managed to go on a roller-coaster ride of hope and despair and wasted their last period searching for something and missing the very thing that makes life worth living, those you love and the things you love doing with them.

3 May

That last piece isn't really fair to all the people who are trying to help and who really care ... I apologize to those who genuinely believe in the remedies they are advocating.

When I was younger I spent hours at various different times trying to do things like move pencils with the power of my mind. I was convinced that it was only my own belief that it was impossible that stopped me from doing it. I must have tried over a hundred times all together. About five years ago I tried something else: I decided I could at least take control of my own body, and I spent about two months, on and off, trying to raise or lower the hairs on my arms, just by concentrating.

Part of me still feels that if I really, really believed that I could cure myself, then I could. But, and this is the problem with religion for me too, you can't fake faith.

I want to stick in a word about Tim today. I've been a bit down lately, and he's so great. He knows me so well, and knows just what to say and how to encourage me. Sometimes I feel sorry that he had to fall in love with me – a somewhat faulty model – but I know that we had no choice. When we first fell in love I said, 'This is too perfect, something is bound to go wrong – like in *Love Story*!'

Hubris.

The gods are jealous.

She really did say that to me, and I think there was a little bit of her that believed that was why we were jinxed, that we were too in love and that for every action there must be a reaction of equal power. If our love was so monumentally beautiful, then there must be something terrible about to happen. Well, it did.

I think both Weeze and I were quite jealous of people with faith. Both of us desperately wanted to believe there was something there, something more, but for whatever reason we couldn't get over the fact that it just didn't seem to add up. I spent three years at university studying religion and came out the other side of it what I would call a hopeful atheist. There was nothing I came across which gave me any sign that religion was more than a fabrication or a method of social control and psychological support. But I wanted it to be true. And now I look back on it, last year I think I prayed every night to God that he would do something, intervene, make it all OK, make the illness and the pain go away. I begged him with tears in my eyes, I screamed at him when I was alone in the house, I called for help, I bared my soul. But Weeze still died. Now, maybe we're not meant to know everything and all will become revealed in the afterlife, and maybe right now Weeze is sitting on a cloud somewhere looking down at the Earth and all of us and shouting down to me, 'Tim, it's OK, it's all here, everything will be made clear later and it's beautiful, so beautiful it makes me want to dance again.' I hope that's the case, but from here, from grief and the darkness, it's difficult to see the point of it all, to even understand faith. I'm not sure I want it now, I don't want to come to it through grief, I'd just be convinced I was going mad. If you've got a plan for me, God, that I'll be able to understand your love and magnificence, could you wait a little while, let me get my head together first, and that way I won't think I'm having a psychotic episode. OK, is it a deal? Let's shake on it, one little mortal hand to one all-encompassing hand which holds all of history in its gentle grip.

8 May

My mood has lifted. I'm super happy at the moment, though I don't really know why. Certainly the response to this site is very helpful – thank you everyone for the lovely messages and emails. Tim and I have also been talking about the future as something more than waiting to get ill.

I've wanted a restaurant for as long as I can remember, and we've been talking about it the last couple of days and know a couple of people who would invest in one maybe . . . I used to be a chef and would love to – well, do everything in the world, really.

I think that maybe if I always keep looking ahead at new projects, the desire to see them completed might keep me alive. Well, it's as good a theory as coffee enemas, I reckon.

Getting really excited about planning something like our ideal restaurant was great – it made me feel really alive. After all, what is life if it's not things to look forward to?

Later

Caitlin said the dreaded words: 'But you're not going to die, are you?' It was strange – I had been gently leading the conversation around to that point, but when it happened I still felt totally unprepared. I asked her what might happen if I never got better. Then I said that everyone dies some time and that if I never got better then one day perhaps I would die. She was quiet for a bit and then said, 'I love my new school hat, Mummy, do you love it?'

I really felt like crying, but I guess it's good that the possibility of my death is out there now, and she can let it sink in for a while and ask questions when she's ready. Tim looked a bit choked up when I told him about the conversation too.

Our friend Jane has found several good books to read with her that deal with the idea of death in ways suitable for her age – one about a leaf, one about dinosaurs and a couple about dealing with feelings afterwards. It's good to know they're around as a resource when we need them. I'm hoping that the gradual pace we're introducing information will mean nothing's a huge shock for her.

I suppose it's like most of parenting – you do your best and then when they're twenty they blame you for everything.

I remember feeling devastated when Weeze told me about that conversation. I welled up as I did throughout the year when I thought about Caitlin. As I still do. It's funny, but with Weeze I only cried a few times, because we were a team, we were pulling together, I was strong for her, she was strong for me and we were getting through it. And so a lot of the time I wasn't that upset about the horrors that she was facing or living with, it was a shared thing. But Caitlin was different. She was, and of course is, my little girl. She is my whole world now, and she always has been, from the moment the midwife said to me, 'Tim, she's crowning, would you like to see your child?' and I looked between Weeze's legs and saw this almond-shaped patch of bloody scalp emerging, I've been smitten and devoted. Mind you, this first view of her had a strange effect on me and I freaked out a bit. I believe I said something like, 'Fuck me, fuck me, fuck, fuckety, fuckfuck, bollocks, shit, fuck . . .' And imagine that going on for another two minutes or so as I wandered up and down the corridor outside the delivery room trying to calm down before going back in to be there for the most amazing thing ever, the birth of my child. I really mean that, I was one of those soppy guys who gets blown away by it. I yabbered on about it to loads of friends who then had children and didn't quite get the whole 'blown away thing', but every now and then I meet some guy who was as knocked out by it as I was and we secretly go all gooey with each other, talk about the overwhelming joy of the first time you hold your child in your arms and look down into the wrinkled package that has stolen something of your soul, of your heart. Then we cough and start talking about football again. Come on, Chelsea! Zola! Zola!

That's why I get so upset – the love I have for Caitlin is so powerful that I can't accept the fact that she will get hurt and feel pain. I know that's life and you can't, nor should you, protect them from everything but, damn, I want to. I can't even take it when we're playing in the park and she goes up to some bigger child and they don't want to play with her. I just want to go over and beat them up, give them a right good slapping. Obviously I don't, so don't be scared of me, I'm nice really.

When I was at school I used to play rugby for the school. One match, when we were about fourteen, we were playing one of our many arch enemies who all looked huge to us. In fact, this was the normal comment when we saw the opposition, no matter who they were: 'They can't be our age, they're enormous, that one there – he's got to be thirty at least.' So this one time we were playing and my best friend at the time, a Scottish kid called Ged, was running down the wing when one of the opposition caught up to him and, rather than tackle him, just chose to punch him on the back of the head. Ged went down like a sack of coal. Now, Ged's dad was a huge six-foot dour Scot, who on seeing this ran on to the pitch and started chasing his son's attacker. The poor kid was petrified – there he was being chased by a furious Scot who was being chased by a referee, two dads from their side and a couple from ours. It was chaos, but damn we laughed, and Ged went totally red and kept shouting, 'Don't Dad, don't Dad, please.' Nothing worse than having your parents fighting your battles for you. But now I've got Caitlin, I'm not sure I could stop myself from hunting down some nasty netballer should she get too physical with my little girl.

12 May

When I was fifteen I had a mysterious post-viral fatigue illness, where I basically lay in bed for six months. I had a year off school and was completely exhausted and depressed. I now think that it was the start of my cancer. Anyway, when I recovered I gave my older sister Dee a book of my thoughts and poems that I had written when ill. Last week she sent me these writings. It's strange, because most of them I can't remember writing at all. Some are very much the work of a fifteen-year-old, but I'm going to write some here because they just seem so prophetic. Bear in mind I didn't discover I had cancer in my head for another nine years.

Something other has taken over my mind,
Slug-like it is oozing over the crenellations of my brain.
It doesn't hurt, but I can feel it if I'm quiet.
A primordial glue, it smears itself onto the insides of me
Suffocating the nerves
Choking my responses
Filling up the cracks
Leaving an impervious sheet of rubber.

However sharp a point you make, your words will bounce off my brain.
Each morning I am vaguely surprised to find I am not dead.

The colour therapist told my mother I mustn't wear black, as it was depressing. So I am in a scarlet nightdress, incongruous against my blue-white skin. My blood has left my body and my mother is trying to paint it back on . . .

Well, that's quite enough of that. Cheerful child, wasn't I?

On a lighter note, Tim and I were interviewed yesterday

by our local TV company, Meridian, for a feature they're doing on this website. It was a bit nerve-racking, but I think it went OK. Caitlin seems to accept everything that's going on – she loved being in front of the cameras. I continue to feel well – took Caitlin swimming this morning with the school and it was brilliant fun – felt like a normal mum enjoying her daughter's excitement.

I think these were the times that Louise most enjoyed throughout her last year, the times when she and Caitlin were together doing mum stuff. I can remember coming into the kitchen one day after I'd been out working somewhere and finding the place full of music and flour. Both my ladies were dancing around madly, Weeze with a mixing bowl in her hand whisking something as she moved, Caitlin with a large skipping rope of dough. I stood in the doorway for a good ten seconds before they even noticed I was there, and when they did they held out their hands and invited me into the dance.

It is good to look back at those times and remember them, because when Louise became very ill she detached herself from Caitlin quite a lot, as if just seeing her coming into her room and knowing she couldn't play with her was too painful. But when she was well the two of them were inseparable. I can remember feeling jealous of how close they were, the way they would look into each other's eyes and a world of knowledge and feelings would pass between them. On a regular basis Weeze would say to me, 'She did it again today! She plucked the words right out of my head.' I saw this happen a couple of times. Out of the blue Caitlin would say something like, 'I'm sure Dee will be all right!' And sure enough, Weeze had been thinking about her sister Dee. I guess it's understandable that kids should be able to pick up on you and what you're thinking, but Caitlin never used to do it with me. In fact, the only person who I've ever had anything like that with was Weeze, of course. I noticed as our relationship went on we could just say one word and a whole sentence or story would be understood. I would know when she was phoning me. I'm sure a lot of people have this with their partners, but it was beautiful for me, like having someone on the same computer network as you, who could dip in and out of your memory files and whose files you could access as well. Computers aren't the most romantic metaphors are they, but you get the idea – just read that last bit and then think of some better, more airy-fairy roses and chocolate images, and you're halfway there.

17 May

Time is a very elastic thing. I've been trying to write down some stuff about my past for Caitlin and trying to work out the dates of when we moved to different houses, but I've come to the conclusion that the facts of a life aren't really important. How you remember things becomes the reality, whether it's true or not. Your thoughts and feelings about life are what make you what you are – whether or not anything is absolutely true doesn't really matter.

So I'm chucking down memories and emotions as they come to me and not worrying about facts. One of the things I remember is that when I was nine or ten I got upset because I wanted to be a writer and thought I would never be one because 'my childhood had been too happy'. I had been told that great art comes from suffering. Now I think that it isn't suffering that helps you create – more that if you are able to write or paint or anything else it helps you through hard times. Not that I'm comparing this to 'great art', but it definitely comes from a need to write at the moment.

Last night we went to dinner at some friends' house and the other couple didn't know that I was ill. It was very nice to have an evening with other people where we talked about things other than me. We had a real laugh about music and normal kinds of conversational stuff. It felt as though I had a night off – particularly as no awkward questions came up – and I was just accepted as a mum.

I'm going through one of those times when I feel so well that it's hard to believe I'm ill and I feel like a fake. I took Caitlin to a birthday party on Friday and had to tell another mum there that I was ill and it sounded so ridiculous coming out of my mouth. I think I'm getting a little better at telling people, though, and after the initial shock they soon realize I'm not going to burst into tears and they visibly relax. Still, this week Tim and I are on TV talking about the website, so soon I probably won't need to tell people myself at all.

And so the media thing started. It wasn't so much a media circus as a media small tent with a couple of people juggling inside it. It was our local news station that came and they were all nice and friendly, but for some reason I felt incredibly nervous. They set everything up in the kitchen and we both did interviews and then they did some set-up shots of me and Weeze going about our everyday lives, which involved me pretending to wash up and Louise pretending to make me a cup of tea. Now, for someone who has acted professionally, directed and teaches drama, I gave one of the most wooden performances ever seen on telly. You'd think they put a rod up my back and told me to move like a robot, whereas Weeze, who had always claimed to be shy and retiring when it came to theatrical matters, blossomed and went into an improv piece that Peter Brook would have been proud of.

When the piece actually came out on telly I was having a meeting at someone's house and it just happened to be on. The woman, who I'd been talking to in a very business-like manner just moments before, saw the piece and started to cry. That more or less put the full-stop to the meeting and I drove home feeling like shit. I was angry at the cancer. I hated the fact that it was fucking up my life in so many ways. Not only in the obvious ways, but that it had such an all-pervading effect – every aspect of my life was tainted by it. I just begged and prayed to have a normal life, a wife who was well and a future that didn't look like dark clouds and lightning.

18 May

A strange morning. I went to see two funeral directors to choose/arrange/pay for my funeral. The first one was lovely – staff sensitive, but had a sense of humour. The son will be doing my funeral because the father is allergic to horses! (Oh yes, I am going to be that dramatic.) The second place was ghastly and reminded me of stepping into a suburban sitting room from the fifties. Me and my friend Jane, who was keeping me company, couldn't wait to leave.

Anyway, in the end I've gone for the works: glass-sided hearse pulled by a team of black-plumed horses and a purple suede-covered casket. I learnt the difference between a casket and a coffin – coffins are much more body-shaped, so I went

85

for a casket. They also had 'green' coffins made of cardboard, which they said were all right as long as it wasn't raining . . . the mind boggles. Also, two 1950s Rolls-Royces for the family to follow in. All very theatrical, but if you're going to be buried you may as well do it in style. I was fine for most of the morning, except when talking about the flowers when I had a sudden image of Tim and Caitlin putting flowers on the coffin.

I know I sound very matter of fact about all this most of the time, but it has to be said that I don't really want to die . . .

And I don't want you to be dead. I can't bear it. Reading through this entry has torn me apart. I can't stem the flow of tears, they come and they come and they come. I have now put the flowers on my wife's coffin. A single black rose from me, a single white rose from Caitlin. I tell you now, there's no harder task, nothing that numbs the mind so comprehensively. It is like an anaesthetic for the senses, too intense for you to take in. The fact that she sorted out all of the arrangements was so like her. Even after she died she was still looking after me. When I had to go down to the funeral directors the day after she died I was read the instructions she'd left and whoever had written them down at the time had obviously put them down word for word, because I could hear her so clearly speaking to me from the grave.

Man, talk about a heavy way of writing this stupid book. I wish I'd read the diary before, then it wouldn't feel like I was being hit by a brick every time I flick to her next entry, and here we are, only in May. If you're reading this in a bound book with a picture of me and Weeze on the front then I managed to slog it out and finish it. Think of the money, Tim, and your poor starving daughter, and buckle down to it. So onwards, friends, let's move forward through the tears.

Tim's page. 19 May

An aching pain consumes my chest when I think of the past or of the future. It slowly tightens, then wells up through my throat, creeps like a slow shiver up my face until it reaches my eyes. I know that tears would cleanse the pain, wash away that level of grief, but I don't want to cry, not yet. There'll be enough crying to wash the whole world clean later, but for now I want to just get by. I want to enjoy being with Weeze.

The interviewer from our local TV station asked me how we keep our spirits up and remain so positive. And this is what came out of my mouth and I think it's how I feel. 'I just don't want to waste time. If I've only got a limited time with Louise I don't want to waste it moping around, I want to really be with her, laugh with her, hold her, make love to her. If we just cried from now on until then it would feel like I started the mourning process before I'd lost anything.' OK, I didn't say it quite that clearly but that's what I meant to say. I think actually I said something like 'Ummm, well, yes, ummm good question, errr ... well it's like, you know, like erm, well my mother always said – life is like a box of chocolates.' I then went on to become a famous American football star, a war hero, a world table tennis champion and I taught Elvis how to dance. No wait that wasn't me that was Forest Gump! Look you get the idea anyway, now stop staring at me in that funny way.

20 May

Sorry if that last entry brought anyone down too much – I'm glad I've done it, but that funeral stuff was very weird; I felt emotionally wrung out for the last two days because of it. Tonight Tim and I are going out to dinner alone for the first time in ages to catch up on how we feel and if we need to get some help around the house or anything, as I am falling over a great deal at the moment.

Tim's last entry made me cry. You see what I mean about our love being too perfect to last? It truly is the stuff of fairytales … Romeo and Juliet stuff. Sometimes I wish he could have fallen in love with someone who was a bit healthier and wouldn't have caused him so much pain. He's practising on the guitar at the moment –'All My Life' by The Beatles. He's been learning it because it's my favourite song, so he can play it to me. I love singing with him. We sit around the kitchen belting out all sorts of things – it's one of the nicest things to be able to share. I don't sing well, but I love it and he's got a great voice. When we first fell in love I bored my family senseless by talking about how brilliant he is all the time, and now I feel like boring you senseless too, but I won't. Instead I'll go and change and put some make-up on and go and stare into his eyes over dinner in a nice restaurant and tell him how much I love him.

Reading that I can see her so clearly coming down the stairs and remember looking at the beauty of her, how exquisite she was. She'd come down looking elegant and serene and she'd take my hand, kiss me, and say, 'Come on then, let's go.' And in six years I never stopped being in awe of her. She was really far too good for me but, hey, everyone's got to be lucky some time, eh? The kitchen was a massively important place for us both. We sang in there, we ate in there, we cooked in there, we danced in there, we even managed to make love in there a couple of times, which was quite a feat seeing as we've got freezing cold slate floors and no curtains, so everyone can see in. I find myself very self-conscious of how Weeze wrote about me, as this lovely, kind, caring, wonderful man. I'm not saying I'm not, I'm just saying it feels immodest of me to include all this stuff, but this is what she wrote so it stays and I'll have to hide my blushes.

However, I should relate a conversation I had with a friend about how I feel about myself. Like many teenagers I was terribly body conscious. I thought I was too fat, too ugly, my hair was weird, I had spots, you know, the usual crap. But when I was with Weeze, she stopped all that. With her I felt beautiful. Not a very manly thing to admit to, I know, but that's how I felt, she made me feel great and beautiful and sexy. For the first time in my life I wasn't embarrassed about the way I looked, I could walk round naked in the house and not have to feel in the slightest bit insecure. And what was it that made me beautiful? Well, love, I guess. Weeze loved me so much that every bit of me became loved and accepted for what it was. In the same way I found it difficult to find flaws with Weeze. I know that she wasn't the most beautiful person ever created, but to me she was. I was looking through eyes which filtered everything through Love. And love makes all things lovely. Feel free to be sick any time you like or just skip on. And it's not just appearance, but the things they do which you can love. A friend's man paints toy soldiers – now, to nearly any normal person this smacks of geekiness in the extreme, but to her it's lovely, sweet, beautiful. Anyway, what's happened to me since Weeze died is that all those old insecurities have come back, it's like being fifteen again when I'm nearly thirty. Crap and a half. It's bad enough when you're young to be riddled with that kind of nonsense but at this age it's just ridiculous, it takes far too much energy and stress.

21 May

I feel fantastic. Tim and I had a really great . . . (no, not that, you dirty-minded people!) chat last night and I feel remotivated about my whole life. We're going to try to get a mother's help to give me a hand with housework and looking after Caitlin over the summer holidays and I'm going back into my darkroom. I got a bit down about my pictures after New York and France, but I think that's because I'm no good at buildings – I much prefer people. So I shall soon be putting a lot more portraits in the gallery – watch this space.

We're also going to re-decorate the house. And I'm going to make Caitlin a wooden box to put special things in. Little creative projects that I can complete are the order of the day, I think. I spent two hours in the darkroom this morning and didn't fall over – although my nose bled all over a couple of prints before I noticed it was bleeding. Still, I feel great having got back in there – I think it was probably more of a mental block than a physical one.

What can I say, I give good chat! That was one of the most positive chats we had over the entire year because we actually sorted a load of crap out. Which is always nice. When faced with death it's often very difficult to get anywhere in discussing problems without someone saying something like, 'Yes, I know, but it all means nothing, it's all pointless, you're going to die.' Or, 'I'm going to die.' Depending on who's speaking. But we managed to talk about all the little things we were having problems with and managed to re-motivate Weeze, if only for a short time. I got really worried when she wasn't working or being creative. I think it was something to do with feeling that as long as she was creating things then there was a point to it all, it all meant something. Maybe I also felt a bit that as long as she was creating and working she couldn't die, but of course she could and did.

25 May

I have an ear infection at the moment which is possibly why I've been falling over so much – I'm going up to Guy's hospital this afternoon, so I shall update this again later. I just realized that it had been a long time since I'd written, so I wanted to say Hi! This site is very important to me – I feel so lucky to have people all over the world rooting for me. I'd like to mention my sister Dee today, as she's done a walk for Cancer Research. She's currently in remission herself from this oh-so-common-and-yet-so-little-talked-about-disease, so she's done a brilliant job to do the walk. WELL DONE, DEE.

It's a strange thing that both sisters should have cancer at the same time. Dee and George, my sister-in-law and her husband, are two of the nicest, kindest and funniest people I know and yet they live with constant disaster hanging over them. Dee got cancer, currently in remission, and George has a heart condition, yet they go on and they get through things and love flows out of them from every pore. People are quite remarkable, aren't they?

26 May

Well, yesterday was fine, if a bit exhausting. One advantage to being terminal is that you don't have to worry about getting bad news when you go up for check-ups — what can he say that's worse? As it was, things don't look too bad. I have an ear infection and my ear will continue to be susceptible to them, so Professor Gleeson said he would insert a grommet in my ear when this infection has cleared up. Otherwise, we talked about cameras and things — I took a couple of photos of his hands. Surgeons, pianists, artists ... all these people's hands are fascinating. Perhaps good illusionists or even pick-pockets too. When I went on holiday to Israel when I was fifteen I stayed in a campsite for a few days and there was a magician-type entertainer there and whenever I saw him, however briefly, he would be wearing my watch. His sleight of hand was really amazing — even when I was alerted to it, he still managed to get it without me stopping him. He had the most interesting hands: large and bony, but also very delicate and feminine. I can't remember his face at all.

The exhausting thing about going up to Guy's is that each time I go I feel the weight of all the previous visits. From when I get off the train at London Bridge I am aware of the memories of going up for numerous scan results, chemotherapy, radiotherapy, hugely traumatic chats with teams of surgeons ... you know the kind of thing. But then, I am relieved I am not having treatment. That probably sounds a bit odd, but it's true.

28 May

Yesterday evening I was out having dinner in a restaurant with some friends and I felt more like crying than I have done for ages. Tim and I went to see the film *Notting Hill* and I identified hugely with the character in the wheelchair. She talks about the randomness of fate and also about how lucky she is 'in many ways' – largely that she has a wonderful relationship with her husband.

Anyway, we went straight from the film into a crowded restaurant where a friend of ours was celebrating her birthday . Everyone looked so young and alive. I felt utterly detached and about fifty years older than everybody there. I spent half the evening trying not to cry, but I knew I would feel even worse if I went home, so I stayed and ate and drank and laughed until I felt better. Which I did. But when I came home I turned this computer on and typed a whole paragraph of 'It's ridiculous'. Then it struck me that that in itself looked ridiculous, so I laughed and went to sleep.

And this goes on. Both of us felt acutely out of sync with our friends and peers. We should have been living a life of growth and health and watching our little girl grow and treasuring her. But we lived in the limbo land of death for more or less five whole years. It wasn't that we grew up and became wise or mature, it was just that we had to face shit that nobody else we knew had ever faced. All around us there were people just getting to grips with life, sorting their heads out and having fun with life, and there we were alone and desperately trying to support each other in the face of disaster. And now that goes on for me, the sense of alienation. I'm a twenty-nine-year-old widower. Mind-blowing. There must be others out there, but it feels a really lonely place to be at the moment. All my friends are still living the way they did at college or school, it's still about drinking and picking up girls or boys and hanging out and all that shit. And I'm a single dad, grieving for a lost wife and wondering what it's all about. And you know what, I don't want to be where I am. I want to have my wife back, and everything back in place.

29 May

Well, I made my first concession to being ill yesterday. I bought a wrist support. I have been falling over more and more recently (up to ten times a day some days), so I thought that I really ought to acknowledge it. I always seem to go down on my left hand and the wrist was beginning to ache, so I bought myself a cool-looking skateboarder's wrist support and am wearing it all the time. It makes me feel a lot more secure. We are also in the process of sorting out some help so that I'm not really on my own much.

It feels like a big step. I mean this diary is where I muse on my mortality, but now I'm beginning to alter my life in practical ways because I'm ill. Up to now I haven't really made any concessions at all — because I haven't really felt ill. But lately I've realized that I have no confidence at all in my stability. I don't carry Caitlin at all really now and I call Tim around when I get out of the bath (well, any excuse to show off now that I've lost some weight!)

Talking (writing?) of baths — a couple of days ago Caitlin was in the bath and she sank a boat she was playing with. She said it was dead and so she buried it under some bubbles.

She then said: 'Let's pray. Dear God and Jesus, please bring back the boat because we miss it.' To which I said, 'If something's really dead, it can't come back though, can it?'

'Well, Jesus died and he came back, so if God wants to he can being people back.'

Thank you, religion. Thank you, school assembly. I've told her that some people believe in God and others don't, but she prays at school, so ... I don't know, I probably worry about stuff too much. On a lighter note, it's half-term holiday and the weather's fabulous, so we're having some great family time and lots of picnics. I urge you all to do the same. I'm off now to lie in the back garden ...

One day around this time Weeze went out on to the patio to sunbathe, and I kissed her and went upstairs to my office. I was restless and couldn't face writing so I took my chair to the window, opened it and let the warm breeze blow over my face as I looked down and watched my wife. I loved watching her when she didn't know I was there. Not in any kind of sick stalker way, I just loved observing her. I put my head on my arms and rested on the windowsill. Without really noticing it had happened I found myself crying and sobbing, the tears soaking into my shirt. I was looking down at her and she was so beautiful but, still, I couldn't help but imagine her dead. I looked down at her and for one of the first times really understood that she was going to die. It hit me like a brick. I knew for certain that at some time I would be looking at Weeze like this and she would be dead. My mind then flipped as I realized she hadn't moved for a good while. I suddenly panicked that she'd gone to sleep down there and simply drifted off. I got up and ran downstairs. I saw her through the kitchen window and she still hadn't moved. I was horror struck – had she died on me, would I go over to her and find her cold? I couldn't actually go out and touch her, so I called quietly for her, but there was no response. I called slightly louder and then she moved. Her head turned towards the house, she was smiling and she said, 'Yes, darling? Is everything OK?' I ran out to her and held her and sobbed. 'What is it?' she asked, but I just asked her to hug me. It was like she had died and I'd got her back, it was sheer relief. But it did make me realize that at some point she wouldn't wake up.

Chapter 6

━━

2 June

Yesterday we went up to see my sister Dee and her family, George, Harry and Twig. The main reason to go up there was to plant a bush in their garden, the idea being that it will always be around to remember me by. It was a good thing to do and Caitlin and everyone helped so it didn't feel too sombre and weighted.

Sometimes I think there's a part of me that thinks that the more preparations I make to die, the less likely it is to actually happen. When Tim and I were trying to get pregnant and I was doing pregnancy tests almost every month, I once bought about ten packets of STs on special offer – the theory being, if for once I'm really resigned and prepared for my period, maybe this time it won't come. It worked – we had Caitlin. Then when she was due to be born everyone said first babies were usually late and I was desperate to have her, so we again decided to be completely unprepared – no hospital bag packed, no nappies in the house – and it worked, she was early.

So this time if I fill the world with memorials, the cosmic joke will be to let me live . . .

3 June

Caitlin had her three-and-a-half-year check yesterday. The health visitor tested her physical and mental development. I've been so wrapped up in myself that I hadn't really thought about her general development much. Tim's better – he's been aware for a while that her diction is pretty lousy, apparently due to the fact that her front teeth stick out because she still has dummies at night. Well, not any more. Yesterday we chucked them out. I felt awful, taking away her main source of comfort, although it will be better for her in the long run. Nevertheless, she had a pretty hard time last night. I so regret giving it to her in the first place.

I think one of the reasons I found it particularly hard was that as Caitlin was throwing herself around the bed crying, it reminded me of when I came off my morphine-based pain-killers a couple of years ago. I got totally hooked on a drug called Palfium after I was ill the first time round and I had a really hard time coming off it. Obviously Caitlin isn't chemically dependent on her dummy, but it just reminded me of one of the hardest things I've ever done. It took a great deal for me to come off it and at first it seemed a little pointless if I was going to get ill again anyway, but actually it was essential to be clear-headed in order to deal with my current situation. All things are for the best.

Caitlin's relationship with Weeze was always very intense. From the moment she first suckled on Weeze's breast they were bonded in a way I can only imagine. Right up until the last few months, Caitlin always looked to Weeze for comfort and guidance. Dad was a big fun guy who larked around and did silly voices. I was very worried that the relationship she had with Weeze would never transfer to me and that she'd feel she had no one to anchor herself to if Weeze was gone. Every night when Weeze was well enough we took it in strict rotation to put Caitlin to bed. On Weeze's nights, Caitlin would happily skip off to bed, looking up adoringly into her mother's eyes, chatting excitedly about what that evening's story was going to be. On my nights, Caitlin would always scream and kick against me, calling out for Weeze, right until I'd actually got her undressed and into bed, when she'd snuggle in defeated and in need of some soothing.

This used to make me sick to my stomach, not because of the actual event itself, as I understood from various friends that kids are often like that with one parent or another, but because of what we were facing. If we couldn't pull it together and become a team, then the future would be even harder. I also ached and still ache with love for Caitlin – even though as I write this she's just turned the shower head on and wrecked the bathroom floor and kitchen ceiling below. She is the most precious thing that has ever happened to me and I'm truly grateful for that, but the responsibility, the pain, that goes with not wanting to fuck her up is immense. Sometimes I want to sit down and cry and cry about what's happened to us. But I can't. I'm desperate not to lose it in front of her. Which, I hasten to add, I know is bad, but it's just a dad thing – you always want to be strong for your kids. I know that's a load of old crap, but it's true, it's how I feel.

Louise's Palfium addiction was possibly the most traumatic time in our married life. She was put on it for something or other, I'm not sure what specifically – headaches, or the pain from the radiotherapy, or her endometrial pain or something – such was the level of pain the poor woman had to put up with. Anyway, as it was thought she was terminal, the doctors at the time prescribed Palfium to help with the pain. From what I understand, it's a highly addictive drug, similar to heroin, which is good at dealing with specific pain. However, Weeze got hooked and hooked in a big way.

The frightening thing was that I hadn't realized how bad the addiction had got until it was far too late – mainly because her personality didn't particularly change when she took it. For some reason I thought that if you were with someone with an addiction they'd be strung out at some points, mellowed at others. But Weeze was still Weeze. The first time I really knew that we had problems was one Saturday night when Weeze realized she didn't have enough of the drug to keep her going through Sunday and that it would be very difficult to get this restricted drug at the weekend. She got nervy and angry, and in the middle of the night I found her rocking backwards and forwards in the bath, going up the walls. I remember saying to her in a jokey way, 'Well, this doesn't look so good, does it?'

Even then she could still laugh and I wrapped her up in a dressing-gown and talked her through the night. It was then that she opened up and cried and cried. She had been exceeding the stated dose of the drug by three times. She was hacking through the stuff – it had become a crutch for her to help her get through each day.

We asked for help and were sent to our local drug rehab centre, and suddenly got to see a whole new side of our sleepy country town. On our first visit a junky ran in the entrance hall shouting madly, then threw up over the carpet. Weeze hated going there, she hated being associated with the kind of people around her. She had got hooked without any knowledge of quite how powerful a drug she was being prescribed, whereas those around her were crack and heroin addicts.

We set out on a programme to slowly reduce, reduce, reduce. It took three months of unbelievable effort on her behalf. Our counsellor told us at the time that it was one of the hardest drugs to come off, and she did it. She shook, she screamed, she cried and she did it. And she never stopped being Weeze, she never got angry with me, she was always a perfect mother, she kept everything going and conquered her addiction. She was a strong, strong woman.

4 June

I've just read yesterday's entry. 'Cleared-headed' – Ha! Today I am having difficulty staying upright. My head feels anything but clear. Fuzzy and spinning and tingling inside would be a far better description. I feel so out of control and frustrated by it. Last night the right side of my face went into spasm for a minute or two, which was rather scary, as I didn't know if it would stop or not. But it did, and feels fine now (still numb, but I'm in control of my muscles).

When we thought I might be in remission, Tim and I

used to reassure each other whenever I had nosebleeds or headaches by saying things like, 'Don't worry, it's probably just an infection /a hot day / lack of sleep, etc., etc.' Now we hug and say, 'Don't worry, it's probably just the cancer.' At least there is no longer anything to be afraid of.

After an entire day characterized by falling over, I can only laugh about it – it does feel as though I'm in some bizarre slapstick comedy. I have spent the evening mentally designing a futuristic cyber-punk wheelchair covered in weird machine parts and spray paint. If only I knew some eccentric inventor to soup it up for me. It feels so ridiculous to feel so well, really, and yet be incapable of walking. I took Caitlin to the playground across the road this afternoon and ended up being helped by a pregnant woman whose baby was due today, but who decided I was in worse shape than her!

To bed to dream of flying, hopefully – much safer than walking.

20 mins later . . .

I've just put Caitlin to bed and, lying in the dark, she said, 'Other mothers aren't like you, are they?' I geared myself up for a question about falling over, and asked her what she meant.

'Other mothers aren't so nice, are they? I bet other mothers aren't so nice as you to their children.' And she rolled over and went to sleep.

Who gives a crap if I'm crap at walking? Tonight I am flying.

5 June

I think the problem is that I feel totally philosophically adjusted to the idea of having cancer and even of dying, but not really of being ill. Death is such a mind-boggling thing to think about that it somewhat obliterated the whole getting ill thing. Not that I feel ill, really, but I can't walk without falling down. Or rather, it is standing still that seems to be the problem. And I'm finding it s-o-o-o-o frustrating. I've kind of got used to falling over now as well, so I feel as though I want to carry on doing ordinary things and just 'pick myself up and start all over again', but I can't risk Caitlin and I also worry a little about cooking and crossing roads.

When my face went numb back in December I found myself waiting for the feeling to come back for ages – it probably took me about a month to stop expecting any change. Now I never think about it. I guess it might be like that with other symptoms, although I still miss chocolate and my taste buds have been up the creek for over a month. Caitlin seems to be pretty used to Mummy falling over already – I expect I will get used to it some time. It just feels like I ought to be able to shake my head clear of it.

As if in compensation for my lack of mobility, my dreams are super-vivid at the moment. When I was twenty-one I stayed in a Buddhist monastery on a silent retreat for a couple of weeks and started lucid dreaming (being able to control one's dreams). The dreams I'm having at the moment feel very real – lots of people I know in them and very vivid colours. I went back to the monastery to cook for a retreat just after Tim and I fell in love, and the theme of the retreat was non-attachment – the idea being that attachment to people inevitably leads to suffering as they are likely to dis-appoint or die. It is true, but surely to live an unattached life is even worse than pain – pain that at least lets you know you are really alive? Even if Tim and Caitlin suffer later on, they know that they loved and were loved to the limits of human capacity.

I've been thinking about this a lot recently. What if I hadn't loved Weeze? Or, at least, what if I hadn't loved her quite so much? I could be going on with my life in a pleasant and jolly manner, unaware of the unbelievable screaming pain that humans are capable of. I know you can't think like that, that it's just stupid. But amongst the tears and nerves and the desperation, these are things that cross your mind. Why did I have to fall in love with her? Why couldn't I have fallen for someone else, some-one nice, friendly, but not as intensely beautiful in mind, body and spirit as Weeze? Then I could go on and not feel like half of me had just been amputated.

The answer, of course, is that I had no choice. I did what I did and would do the same again at the drop of a hat, but you do wonder about it, and you do get angry. Not at Weeze or anyone, really, you just do, and when you scream in the middle of the night 'I wish I'd never loved her!' you then beat yourself up with guilt. But that's what happens. I loved her, she got ill, she died and now I'm leading a living death without her. I know I'll get through and things will get better. But you do think of a million things at the same time which send your mind spinning trying to cope with the pain, the loss. Ahhhhggg!

The thing which amuses me about this entry is that it shows the basic difference between me and Weeze. About the same time as Weeze was in *her* monastery, I was in a Tibetan Buddhist monastery in Scotland. Now, where Weeze got up at four every morning and kept her vow of silence and actually ended up seeing a vision in a tree, I forgot to take my alarm clock. Everything at the temple happened before six in the morning and being a young lad, used to sleeping in, without an alarm clock I was lost. At somewhere around eleven in the morning I would stir, about twelve I'd manage to crawl out of the bed and by one I was up and ready for the day. Just in time to catch the last meal of the day. I basically missed everything. I was there at the time they were opening and dedicating the temple, so each morning of the week I managed to sleep through rare lama dancing, never-before-seen-outside-Tibet rituals, extraordinary exhibitions of chanting and meditation. Even when I was awake I found myself unable to chill out and relax. My meditation was poor, my commitment was non-existent. I also found the monks' and sisters' laid-back attitudes annoying. Everything was so slow it drove me crazy.

In the end I only lasted four days before I phoned my mum up one morning and asked her to phone the office in the big house in twenty minutes' time. I duly headed off for a walk round the shop selling incense and scriptures. Sure enough, twenty minutes later a beautiful nun found me and in her whispered hushed tones informed me I had a phone call. I went into the office and picked up the phone.

'No, really, no, no. OK, I understand. OK, I'll come as soon as I can. What a shame, I was loving it here, it's so peaceful. OK, thanks Mum. I love you, take care. I'll be home soon.'

I put the phone down on my bewildered mother and turned to the assembled kind and caring spiritual friends around me. They all looked concerned, I looked sad. They ordered me a taxi and within the hour I was on my way home, my heart leaping with joy, feeling like I'd been released from prison. Before I left, though, I had a moment of guilt and headed into the temple to say a final prayer. For the first time since I'd been there the wonderful red and gold temple was empty and I was the only one in there. I sat in the lotus position, looking up at the thousand golden Buddhas, and contemplated why I'd failed to find enlightenment. No answer came and after five minutes I felt itchy and excited about leaving. I looked round and, still being alone, I danced down the aisle of the temple singing at the top of my voice 'I Feel Good' by James Brown. It was only when I reached the front of the temple that I realized I was not in fact alone, but that two holy men were sitting in silence at the front, obscured from my view by a large prayer wheel. They both looked up at this noisy whirling dervish and smiled big Tibetan smiles, truly beautiful, but it just confirmed my feelings that this wasn't the right place for me and off I headed home, another spiritual journey ending in failure.

Weeze was naturally spiritual, although she didn't really have any specific faith, and positively didn't believe in the Christian concept of God. She had a spirituality not limited by creeds. She just was a spiritual person and everyone knew it when they came into contact with her. I'm not sure I can really describe it any better than that. During my life I've come across four people who for me summed up what being a spiritual person is – people who truly live a spiritual life, don't just go through the motions, are able to transcend the pettiness that religion imposes and see the 'real' world. One was a monk up at the monastery, one was a Catholic priest who was a lecturer at my college, the third was a rabbi and the last was Weeze. Sounds like a gag, doesn't it? 'All right, there was a rabbi, a priest, a buddhist monk and woman dying of cancer.' OK, not a very funny joke, but you get the idea. These people – none of whom except Weeze would even remember meeting me – have been very influential in my life and the way I look at it. They all exuded love and peace and that was where their religion began and ended. The finer points of belief meant nothing, the only thing was love, the love of all things. Once you can truly do that, everything else falls into place. I'm nowhere near there, but that's what I aspire to. If my monk friend is right, give me a few more lifetimes as the wheel turns and, who knows, maybe I'll be able to actually do what I'd like to be able to do.

7 June

I spoke to my surgeon at Guy's hospital this morning and he's going to put a grommet in my ear on Thursday. It is strange to think that this is my first hospital procedure since my scan six months ago. Most people assume that I'm in and out of hospital all the time and on all sorts of drugs.

The balance is no better and apparently the time it takes to adjust to it is anything up to a year, so I shan't hold my breath. We've been recommended to put an extra rail along the staircase and by the bath. I feel resentful towards the cancer for the first time in absolutely ages about this. Why should we have to mess about with our lovely house to accommodate this frustrating new turn of events. For now, I travel up and down the stairs crawling and bumping on my bottom, which Caitlin thinks is hilarious, as she is now such a big girl and walks like an adult.

The grommet operation involves a short general anaesthetic, but I shall be out that day. I am so glad I don't spend any regular time in hospital. I'm not scared of hospitals or anything, but they do remind me of times filled with pain and loneliness. I see no reason to delve into my memories of chemotherapy – it certainly wouldn't help anyone currently facing it. Suffice to say it was not fun, and I shall be glad not to be staying the night on Thursday.

9 June

I've just promised a friend, who is a hard-core Christian, that I will go and see a healing couple. They live very close and are well known locally and I have nothing to lose, I suppose. The main reason I've agreed to go is that he speaks in tongues. I've never heard speaking in tongues in real life and I'm fascinated. I guess I'm curious as to what they'll do or say as well. I'm not expecting anything from it, but have given my word to my friend that I will go – I did say for the entertainment if nothing else – so I shall. Watch this space.

I'm going to the cinema tonight to take my mind off tomorrow – I'm a bit nervous, not about the operation, but just about going into hospital. Still, at least you get ironed sheets in hospital, which are unheard of around here. If I had unlimited funds and servants, I would have clean ironed sheets every day. As it is, I stretch the sheets as tight as I can and pretend they're ironed. Life, as they say, is too short to iron much other than shirts.

I always dreaded hospital much more than Weeze. For me, every time she faced an operation, however small it was, I thought it was just another chance that I could lose her. And then I knew I would have to leave her and return home to our bed alone, knowing that she was alone in a strange place with people around her that didn't love her like I did. The worst one, of course, was the big operation she had to remove the cancer the first time. It was a massive operation where they removed her face, debulked the tumour and then stitched her up again.

A week before the op I was taken aside by a sweet doctor and asked if I'd videoed Weeze for Caitlin. I wasn't really clear why he was asking me this. It was only when he told me that his father had died and he had some film of him that gave him some comfort, that I realized he was saying that the operation could go wrong and she might actually not make it through. It destroyed me.

We were told there was a reasonable chance she might be blind afterwards and so the night before I took her into hospital she spent the longest time just looking at my face, feeling every bump with her hands, looking into my eyes as if trying to sear it into her memory. She did the same with Caitlin. The next day I had to take her into the hospital and leave her there alone to face the night and whatever demons might be haunting her about the next morning's events. On the way up to King's I couldn't stop myself crying. I turned to her and said, 'Weeze, I'm really sorry, but I don't think I'll be able to say goodbye. I think I'd break down.'

So we made a pact. I'd go up to the ward, settle her down, make sure everything was OK and then, at a suitable moment, I'd simply say I was going for a cup of tea and that would be it – I'd leave. And that was exactly what I did. I unpacked her stuff, I got her tucked up in bed, helped her fill out her forms, kissed her hands a little and then stood up, stretched as casually as I could and looked down at her.

'I'm a bit thirsty, I think I'll go and get a tea.'

She smiled up at me so bravely and said, 'OK, Tig, you do that. I love you.'

I turned and walked away from her, not really knowing

if I'd ever see her alive again. I got about ten steps down the corridor out of her view before I started to cry, and I kept on walking. I fought every urge in my body to go back and hug her. I kept on walking, through the tears, out of the hospital, into the chilly, rainy night and sat in the car and sobbed and sobbed. She was my everything and she looked so fragile, so helpless. I must have sat in the car looking up at the hospital for a good hour before I eventually went into an automatic pilot mode, started the car and drove home.

I don't remember anything of the next twenty-four hours. I know I went home, I know my mother looked after Caitlin, I know I went for a walk during the day, I know I bumped into my father-in-law in Habitat and was unable to really talk about what was going on as we spoke. Then I started looking at the clock. It was well past the eight hours I'd been told the op would last, and still there'd been no phone call. Eventually I phoned and was put through to Professor Gleeson, still in surgery. He told me the op had been a success and that they were just reconstructing her. I was still numb. She'd made it through. I hugged our tiny baby daughter.

That was what hospital meant to me every time after that, it meant having your heart ripped out. Whenever she was told she had to go in and stay over my first reaction was always to cry. As you can tell, I cry a lot.

11 June

Hospital was fine, in the event. My ear hurts a lot at the moment, but will apparently settle down. Yesterday I felt grumpy and hung-over from the anaesthetic, as well as premenstrual, so I wasn't much fun to be around. Today I feel much more positive, however. I am in the mood for an image change and want to feel more glamorous, so I bought some purple nail polish and painted my toes. I suppose I should say toenails, but in my case it really is more like toes. I'm not very good at all the girlie stuff. I am impatient and not practised at make-up and hair and suchlike. My mother never really wore much make-up and my teenage years were spent dyeing my hair black and seeing how much black mascara and eyeliner my eyes could take and still manage to open. So I am not confident as a would-be well made-up adult. I have, however, bought a ruinously expensive hat, which should detract from my smudgy eyes. I'm not sure where I'm going to go, in my finery, but recently I have strong urges to be excessive and extravagant in general. There's a poem called 'When I'm old I'll wear purple' and I feel a little like that. I have nothing to lose or nothing to fear in terms of being seen as ridiculous or eccentric, so I am on the verge of beginning to act a little wild . . .

I guess some of that has rubbed off on me. As I type this I'm looking down at my fingernails painted with her purple nail polish. In Tunbridge Wells, men don't wear nail polish, let alone bright purple nail polish. I just figure it looks cool, and I think everyone else around me thinks I'm wearing it because I'm in the depths of mourning and so not quite in my right mind. Maybe they're right, but it's hardly the most rebellious thing in the world to do, is it? I'm also growing a beard. I guess maybe I'm trying to counterbalance the girliness of the nail polish. Who cares, what it really comes down to is that I don't have to impress anyone or be anything for anyone any more. I've had the great love of my life, I'm not trying to pull anyone, and the only person I ever cared about how I looked for has gone, so for a little while I might as well play with how I look – see if I can't reinvent myself as a butch drag queen. Forgive me, Caitlin, it's probably just a phase and I'll grow out of it before your friends start calling you names because you've got a crap weird dad. In my head I'd love to promote this book on 'Richard and Judy' in full drag. Time to call my counsellor again, perhaps. Still, you've got to laugh, haven't you?

13 June

My computer is broken. The lovely Mac laptop I have is crashing almost continuously, so I am writing this on Tim's iMac. Tim didn't have my website software on his, so I've been incommunicado for a couple of days, and it made me realize how important the site is to me. I felt really cut off without the means to talk to all of you and I felt as though I wasn't sure what I was doing. This diary has become much more than an outlet for my emotions – it is also what I do. Still, it is a little scary to be so reliant on technology – at the mercy of the millennium bug, etc.

14 June

I have been looking back over this diary a bit this morning and a few things occur to me. Firstly, that time passes so fast. It is now pretty much six months since I was given the prognosis and I expected to achieve a lot more, I think. Or, I expected to have done more practical stuff anyway. The recipe book, for example, and the letters to Caitlin. I have started writing a bit for Caitlin in her own special book because although I think this diary will be good for her to read, I think she will want something that was written just for her, and not shared with the world. I thought I would start sticking the odd recipe on here in case I don't get around to writing a book of them.

The weather has finally cleared, after weeks of clouds, and the effect on my mood is, as usual, immediate. I am re-motivated and energized. Just to update everyone – the restaurant idea I aired recently is not going to happen. The amount I am falling over made me realize I am not physically up to such a huge project; instead my energies are focused on re-decorating our house. A friend called Lorraine who is an interior decorator is doing wonderful things – including a cloudscape on our bedroom ceiling.

I am also going to Harvey Nichols in London this week to splurge some money on clothes – I have the urge to look absolutely fabulous. I'm going to have a huge birthday party this year (August) – it will probably be the last one I have where I am well enough to eat, drink and make merry, so I shall. I feel at the moment I am going through a time of reassessment of my aims – I want to make sure that I am still doing all that I want to be doing. There is a renewed feeling of urgency for some reason. I phoned my younger sister – the one who isn't speaking to me – and left a message on her answerphone, but she hasn't rung back. I feel like I did when I first found out – that I want to make sure any loose ends are tied up . . . Anyway, I've rambled on enough today, so I shall go and try to put this up now.

And what of Anthea, Weeze's younger sister? Well, let's just say everyone has to deal with the things they do and the things they don't do. You have to take responsibility for your life and actions, and live with the decisions you make. She has a lot of her own problems, both health-wise and with her husband, who is very ill himself, and I feel she just couldn't face Weeze's illness – so she didn't. I swore for a long time I wouldn't speak to her again, but death has a strange way of mellowing you and now I feel neither hate nor love for her, just a bit sad that she missed out on knowing Weeze right at the end.

Anthea was by no means the only person who couldn't face the illness. Several of our good friends stopped getting in contact and would occasionally cross the road to avoid talking to us about it. This wasn't because they didn't like us, or because they were insensitive, it was often because they were too sensitive. They couldn't handle the feelings of grief and pain they felt when they talked to us, even when we were in up moods. No one should feel bad about this – I honestly don't know how I'd have responded in their place. Most of these people were our age or younger and I guess the last thing you want is to be made aware of your own mortality when your adult life is effectively just starting.

16 June

Well, I went to see the healing bloke who speaks in tongues. It is lucky that I hadn't got excited about the prospect of being cured, as now he only heals one-to-one in 'exceptional cases' and otherwise does healing ministry when invited to by churches. I was offered healing by a lady he is training, but she is only available during school holidays. This proves once again, I think, how disappointing it can be if you get your hopes up. Still, I think Tim was a little relieved, as he said that people who speak in tongues can be a little too heavy on the 'out demons' front, which may have been scary.

I am getting really fed up with feeling so helpless re. falling over. This morning I joked to Tim about quitting while I was ahead, as months of watching my life slowly being taken away from me doesn't really appeal. I mentioned shooting myself at midnight on stage at my birthday party, so he said any time it looked like I was going to make a speech he would rugby tackle me to the ground. I'll emphasize that this was a joke – I'm just sharing things that occur to me. At least the frustration gives me energy, which is a good way to channel it, I think. So, I'm off to sample the delights of Sainsbury's – which I do actually quite enjoy these days!

19 June

It's suddenly come back. That whole intensity of how wonderful life is thing that is nature's way of compensating one for dying. I feel FANTASTIC. It comes and goes, but I definitely have it now – when the knowledge that you have a limited time seems like a bonus – like you're the only person around who can really appreciate life and really live for the joy of each day . . .

I feel lucky, oh so lucky,
I feel pretty and witty and gay (in a manner of speaking, and purely to quote *West Side Story*, you understand),
And I pity any girl who isn't me today.

It reminds me of when I was pregnant and when I ate things that I really craved they tasted amazingly intense. I remember telling Tim that I felt sorry for him that he couldn't experience that intensity. Today I feel pity for anyone who does not know this intensity, the value of this life. Well, there has to be the odd day of compensation for the predicament I'm in. Or perhaps the tumour has just entered my brain and I've gone bonkers – if so, it's a nice way to go! My message for the day is to urge everyone who reads this to go out and do something spontaneous and fun that you wouldn't normally do. Carpe Diem.

Later on that day . . .

All hail the Queen of Mood Swings. Have just read that last bit back and it seems to have been written by someone else. I get worried about this diary being too depressing to read, so I often write it when I'm in a good mood, and leave it for a day when I'm not. In the interest of honesty and to reassure everyone that I'm not a saint who's dealing with this fabulously all the time, I thought I'd stick a few words down tonight. Tonight I am a bitter, bad-tempered, frustrated, weepy, miserable woman. I've been horrible to Tim today, whom I seem to expect to be unfailingly good-humoured throughout everything that happens. I don't know what I'm doing with my life. I'm lost. I know it's expected to feel all these things sometimes, and I know I'll probably feel better tomorrow, but right now that doesn't seem to help. Maybe a belief in God gives you someone to get angry with who isn't your long-suffering husband. I'm going to bed now and I hope I'll wake up happier.

I can't remember her ever getting angry with me, so either I'm an insensitive man who just didn't notice or her idea of being angry with someone was so mild that it passed off as being mild annoyance, and I can live with that. Over the whole last year I probably opened up to her only a couple of times and the reason was that it seemed to affect her physically. If she knew that I was feeling bad or suffering or unhappy about the way we'd handled something, she'd visibly sink. Within an hour or so she would be feeling sick, and could often go down for several days. However you phrased it, it would sound like a criticism of her, because she was the one with cancer and if there were problems related to our lives with the illness she always thought of it as being her fault. Silly cow.

It also made it very difficult for me though, because certain things would cause me stress or anxiety and normally Weeze would have been the first person I'd have talked it through with, but suddenly I couldn't. I was alone and having to grow up, and that's remarkably difficult for a big kid like me who's basically been looked after all his life. That being said, we still talked loads about stuff, but it was very much on a matter-of-fact level. She was allowed to get emotional and a lot of the time I had to be strong. I don't look back on it as me being hard done by in any way – I think that I was glad to be able to be the strong one for once in our married life.

20 June

Apologies for that last entry. I did wake up in a better mood. I don't actually feel that shitty very often (honest, guv). Anyway, today I am me once again and much happier. For all the lows in my life, I wouldn't have it any other way, really. A life of monotony would be far too boring for me. As I re-read yesterday's entry it struck me that it was a bit like my life of illness and love; you could read it and think how awful, but look at the morning's entry. What a ride!

21 June

Monday morning. Back to life, back to reality. The decorating moves on apace. The dining-room looks like a set from the 'Tempest' – all moody blues washed into each other – and the sitting-room is currently being painted red and gold – a 'distressed nineteenth-century brothel' look. Tim was heavily influenced by L'Hotel in Paris where we stayed and I'm up for anything dramatic and over-the-top.

A really lazy, easy recipe, that is delicious:

Take one tub of vanilla Haagen-Dazs out of the freezer and leave it to soften slightly. Crush half a bag of amaretti biscuits with the end of a rolling pin. (I don't know what size bag of biscuits they have in the States, but I'm sure you can use your imagination.) Mix together quickly, then stuff back in the ice-cream tub and re-freeze. There will be some that doesn't fit back in – this is known as Chef's Perks.

Then skin some peaches by plunging into boiling water for a minute or two. Halving them is too much hassle when they're skinless and slippery, so stick them in an ovenproof bowl with a lid and some caster sugar and water. You can add raspberries (sieved if you're feeling posh), or a vanilla pod or a cinnamon stick. Bake for about forty minutes – or for however long the oven is on for the first course. They're easy – just check to make sure they aren't drying out.

Serve with the ice cream. The ice cream is also great alone or with any number of other things. One thing, though –

make it on the day you're going to eat it or the amaretti biscuits go a bit soft. Enjoy!

This is just one of a thousand recipes that helped me go from a svelte young 32-inch-waisted twenty-two-year-old to a somewhat less than svelte 36-inch-waisted twenty-nine-year-old. OK, I can squeeze into a pair of 34s if I really try, but after a while I start losing feeling in my legs and my feet feel like jelly. I blame Weeze for a lot of the outward signs of my increasing age. Especially for my gradual but nevertheless present loss of hair. When we got together I looked a bit like a majestic lion, with long blond hair. And this had been how I'd looked for ever. Well, I had a brief period presenting children's telly when I was at college and they cut all my hair off, but apart from that six months I've always had this great mane. That is until summer 1998 when I wandered into my local Toni and Guy hairdressers and told them told cut it all off. The guy smiled his pants off, put Beck's song 'Devil Haircut' on the stereo and hacked it all away, leaving me shorn and shocked.

When I came back to the house I realized my shock was as nothing compared to that I'd inflicted on Weeze. I got right into the back garden, right up close to her, before she realized who I was. She jumped nearly three feet in the air and ran into the house squeaking. Gradually she eased herself back into the garden and tried to be more positive about the radical change of image.

'I've never really seen your face, whatever possessed you to do it?'

OK, not quite as positive as I'd hoped, but then maybe I should have warned her. Caitlin was the most positive of anyone – 'Daddy's hair's all gone, I love you, Daddy.'

Over the following week Weeze gradually came round to the idea of this new man she was living with. It amazed me how much of an impact such a small thing as cutting all your hair off can have. It wasn't just Weeze, it was everywhere, and not all negative by any means. I started getting more work. For some reason people saw me as a more responsible grown up, someone who could be trusted with projects. Before, people would often come up to me at *Time Out* and say things like, 'Oh, Tim, could you just run this down to John on the third floor, he's the one with . . . oh, don't worry I'll do it.' It was as if, having long hair, I was incapable of rational thought. It may also have had something to do with people thinking I was stoned all the time. A woman down in the computer department at the magazine said when she saw my new hair, 'Blimey, Tim, all your hair gone, you'll stop getting stoned next.' This blew me away because of all the people I know I'm the most anti-drugs, but there you go, guys, a lesson for all of us.

Weeze was the most extreme though. One evening she came into the living room where I was chilling out in front of the telly, let out a little scream and dropped her tea. In the five minutes since she'd last seen me, she had forgotten I now had short hair and had come into the room to find a stranger casually reposed on her sofa. We laughed loads, then I cleaned up the tea. Apparently it was my fault.

22 June

Today I have been really naughty. I had a bath whilst alone in the house and then went down to the High Street alone. It felt deliciously illicit, like sneaking out after dark when you're a teenager. I miss being alone sometimes and feel I am too old (or too young) to be babysat all the time.

I have a nose and possibly an ear infection and so am on antibiotics. Thus ends Louise, not with a bang but with a series of irritating little whimpers . . .

I got some great clothes, by the way, when I went shopping on Friday, and I feel rather elegant, if I say so myself. I never know when people give me compliments these days whether they mean 'you look good for a dying-of-cancer-type-bird' or whether they really mean that I look good. Not much way of knowing, I don't think. I suppose I shouldn't care, that I should be less bothered about superficial beauty than others of my age, but I feel I have to get everything packed in. Who knows, I might have reached my physical peak at thirty-five. Although I rather suspect I looked my best at fifteen. That's when I first met Tim – although we both needed a good six or seven years of doing other things before we were ready to go out with each other. I don't know where this is going, so I'll leave it for now. Au revoir.

I can tell you what people meant, they meant she looked fabulous, for anyone. In her last year, before she got really ill, I think she looked as beautiful as she ever looked. She wore wonderful clothes, her body was in great shape, her hair was divine and she had a confidence about her that was irresistible. The day after her big operation I went up to King's to see my wife, the one who survived. I headed for intensive care and – here's the thing – no one told me what to expect, no one stopped me for a second even and said, 'You know this is not going to look good, don't you?' I was so excited about seeing her that it hadn't occurred to me what a twelve-hour operation would look like in physical terms.

I entered intensive care and the whole place freaked me out. Machines everywhere keeping people barely alive. I walked past Weeze, so convinced that it couldn't be her. I couldn't reconcile in my mind the thing lying in bay three with the wife I'd left in the ward upstairs two days before. She looked like something out of a Frankenstein movie, like some creature pieced together from bits of other people. That, or as if she'd been beaten up by a gang of bikers with chains. There were tubes, stitches, machines beeping, blood, mucus, bruising and some-where under all that was Weeze. When I'd actually taken it in that it was actually Weeze, I sat next to her and held her hand. No response at all from her – she was in a deep coma. I lasted about two minutes before it all became too much for me and I could no longer talk through the lump in my throat. I patted her and bolted for the door. I cried and cried in my dad's arms out in the corridor. It devastated me totally. It was the only thing over the whole time that I just wanted to run away from. Really run away from. Every part of my body screamed, 'Run, leave it all behind, it's too much.' But that's the thing you can't do, you can't run away, you can't not face up to things.

And she did get better. Slowly she began to look normal again and slowly she came back to me. And here's the funny thing – she came back prettier. Some of the tumour had grown into her nose so Prof had to take it out. The nose he gave her wasn't that different really, just a little smaller and a bit cuter. She always said that it was an extreme way to go about getting a nose job. Anyway, she looked gorgeous.

24 June

'You see things vacationing on a motorcycle in a way that is completely different from any other. In a car you're always in a compartment, and because you're used to it you don't realize that through the car window everything you see is just more TV. You're a passive observer and it is all moving by you boringly in a frame.

On a cycle the frame is gone. You're completely in contact with it all. You're in scene, not just watching it any more, and the sense of presence is overwhelming. That concrete whizzing by five inches from your foot is the real thing, the same stuff you walk on, it's right there, so blurred you can't focus on it, yet you can put your foot down and touch it anytime, and the whole thing, the whole experience, is never removed from the immediate consciousness.' Robert M. Pirsig

In illness, confronting death, the protection of the car is removed and life is raw and real. I'm re-reading *Zen and the Art of Motorcycle Maintenance*. I last read it when I was fourteen or fifteen and the main thing I remember about it is the that-book-has-changed-my-life feeling.

A while ago I was thinking about all the books I wanted to read, the classics I thought I would get round to eventually. But I actually want to re-read things that have affected me. I want to consolidate this personality that I have, to make sure I know who I am. I think that's why I'm not that bothered about travelling; other people assume I must want to see the world, but actually I want to learn my immediate neighbourhood by heart and revisit all the houses and schools I have lived in and attended. It's like I want to have a firm grasp of who I am and what I have done on this Earth.

I hope that makes sense. I'm working it out as I write. That's mostly how I do this page – it's my time to work out how I'm feeling about stuff. The rest of the time I'm busy living my life. There's a song by Kenny Rodgers (believe it or not) that I often find myself singing as I call up this page – 'I just checked in to see what condition my condition was in'. It feels like that in a way – I use the website to find out how I'm doing, as you guys reading it do.

26 June

A few symptoms to report. Tinnitus. This is very irritating and changes frequency enough to draw my attention. I considered an elaborate joke for Tim's benefit which involved pieces of paper with dots and dashes on them and talk of receiving encoded messages from aliens / world governments / ghosts, etc. Then I decided I might really go mad soon enough, so perhaps it wasn't in the best possible taste. Not that that has stopped me so far. I also have some pain in the back of my throat and my right eye feels slow, as though it is being dragged down. It all looks normal as yet.

I had a long conversation with Professor Gleeson yesterday, who is so lovely and caring. There are various things they can do to deal with some of my symptoms as they occur: facial tucks to help if my face drops, prism glasses to help my slow eye. He said a zimmer frame wouldn't be elegant enough for me – ahh, a doctor who understands.

On that subject, my district nurse is coming round to assess my needs on Monday. She has ordered me a tripod walking stick and can show me all the marvellous gadgets available to make my home look like that of a ninety-two-year-old. Whoopee. Professor Gleeson didn't think the symptoms represented central growth, only peripheral. Which I guess means I'm not going to die imminently.

On a lighter note, my darling daughter won her first race at school sports day. We are so proud. We are so proud. She rode home on Tim's shoulders waving her fists in the air and shouting 'winner' with a huge grin on her face. These are the moments we live for.

And then some. I couldn't believe it as I watched my little three-year-old girl line up for her first race. My heart was in my mouth. She looked tiny at the end of the school playing field. All the dads were standing round trying to pretend that it didn't mean anything, but you could tell by the clenched jaws that everyone secretly wanted their child to pummel all the others into the ground. Then the starter's gun banged and off they went. Ten pairs of little legs started staggering at top speed down towards the winning tape. Twenty parents cheered and whooped it up. There was a certain quiet confidence about the fathers of the boys, but they needn't have been so smug, they all crumbled in the wake of two mighty athletes – Caitlin and her best friend India. They both put their heads down and headed for the ultimate prize, a lolly and a sticker. Where all the others wobbled sideways, or fell over, or just stopped to pick some flowers and then had a quick nap, Caitlin and India were focused and determined. It was touch and go, nip and tuck all the way. Every five yards the lead changed and as they entered the last three feet they were neck and neck, not an inch between them.

Then, in a final touch of genius, Caitlin's arm went up and she handed off her best friend, pushing her to the ground as she gritted her teeth and took the ribbon.

I found it hard not to be over-proud of my little hero and tried to console the other losing parents, to say things like 'It doesn't really matter does it?' and 'Better luck next year', but I couldn't stop myself from jumping up and down screaming, 'Yes! In your face! In your face! I won . . . I mean, she won . . .' I've rarely, if ever, felt so over the moon. It wasn't just because Caitlin had won a glorious victory, but also because Weeze had been there to see it. It was one of those landmark events that is what having a kid is about and one which Weeze got to participate in.

28 June

Uh-oh, I feel a rant coming on. And this morning's subject, my friends, is God. Well, not God, I have nothing to argue with there, but People Who Wish to Save Me. I would like to clear up a couple of things. The first is that my lack of belief is not to be confused with a lack of information. Being told that God heals people, or that his Son is called Jesus, is not going to give me faith. If God wants me for his sunbeam, it will be done by Grace and Revelation, not by the faith of others. What I really don't get is why it is the people who have the most faith who seem to be so bothered about my dying. Surely they should have utter faith in God's master plan. God will heal me if it is best for the Universal plan or see me die if it isn't.

Hear Ye: The day I declare on this website that Jesus is my personal saviour is the day you can know that I fear death.

And I do now feel as though I'm dying. Not imminently, but it is no longer the case that 'if I hadn't seen the scan I wouldn't believe I had cancer', as I said earlier. I now feel ill. My eyesight is very strange – it's like living in a movie where someone has been drugged and everything goes weird. I'm tired and feeling some pain in my mouth ... but I'm having my hair cut this afternoon to cheer me up after the district nurse's visit, so life ain't all bad. I shall let you know what colour my hair is later on ...

Later on ...

Thank you everyone who responded to this morning's message. I was feeling a little low and as a result was perhaps too harsh on those religious well-wishers who really are trying to help me so much. I do appreciate the love I receive from everyone.

I went out with my new tripod walking stick this afternoon and felt very angry with it (the poor inanimate object). It slows me down a lot and seemed to get in the way as often as it helped. Patience and practice, I suppose. My hair was meant to be shockingly blonde, but has come out as rather naff blonde highlights – my hairdresser is a great bloke, but I seem to have an inability to communicate with the species! Oh well, I shall go back soon and go radically bleached – compensating for feeling about eighty years old with the stick!

29 June

I am massively, but massively buzzed. I've had the most fabulous day. Saw beyond the physical limitations ... went on a really high swing in the playground this afternoon and it felt as though I were flying. I was ageless and physically free and it was FANTASTIC. I sang.

Also just come back from seeing the film The Matrix. *Appalling dialogue aside, I got a similar buzz from it to that of* Phenomenon *— the sudden clear insight that the cancer is a gift and that I can see and feel powerful and invincible. Kind of like I want to do physically impossible things because I know that it's all right and I cannot be harmed or feel fear. Someone show me a truckload of movies before I die. I am flying and feel immortal.*

Chapter 7

—

1 July

Remember when the first day of the month was exciting? I want to stop the clock but, as it says in my pocket *Rubaiyat*:

> 'The moving finger writes; and, having writ,
> Moves on: nor all thy Piety nor Wit
> Shall lure it back to cancel half a Line,
> Nor all thy Tears wash out a Word of it.'

I used to know most of it by heart and a lot of such stuff comes back to me at the moment. I feel that as my physical reality gets harder, I retreat into a mental one a little. When I was having chemotherapy I spent hours creating a world of beauty and tranquillity in my head as a refuge – a place to remove myself from that which I found almost unbearable. It is a place I am returning to occasionally now. I imagine that everyone has similar kinds of fantasy – probably what everyone pictures when they say the word 'heaven'. Mine is built up of images from books and fairytales and things that have entered my subconscious over the years. There are strange medieval buildings to explore and the Hanging Gardens of Babylon exist there. It never rains, needless to say.

I need it at the moment, because things are getting uncomfortable. Last night I couldn't sleep because I had a really strong image of Caitlin waking up in the night and calling for me and Tim having to remind her that I was dead. It was like watching a horribly invasive documentary – you want not to watch it, you think it's wrong to have it filmed, you know it doesn't do anyone any good to watch it, yet it is on and you can't shut it out. It upsets me to think about the Afterwards, and I don't think it is constructive, so mostly I don't think about it. It is only when we are drifting off to sleep and our mind's defences relax, that these things can creep in. Now, awake again, I am back in the present, enjoying the things I have . . .

'Ah, fill the cup: – what boots it to repeat
How Time is slipping underneath our Feet:
Unborn TOMORROW, and dead YESTERDAY,
Why fret about them if TODAY be sweet!'
(The Rubaiyat of Omar Khayyam trans. Edward Fitzgerald)

Everyone should have a wife who can quote from obscure Middle Eastern texts at the drop of a hat! Man, that was a beautiful piece of writing, beautiful and sad. So far the scene from her dream hasn't come true. Caitlin and I stumble through the days as best we can. Well, I stumble through the days, but she seems radiant and glowing, a strong and intelligent little girl.

The other day she came running shouting out, 'Mummy? Mummy? I mean, Daddy? Daddy?' She laughed at her mistake and when she found me in the kitchen she was still laughing and said, 'I called you Mummy, but you're not a Mummy, you're a Daddy. Aren't I silly?' She than ran up to me and gave me the biggest hug. 'You're the warmest daddy in the whole world, aren't you, Daddy? Now come and see what I've done.'

And we were off, hand in hand up the stairs to see what new havoc she'd wreaked over our bathroom.

It's funny that when Weeze described Heaven she said, 'It never rains, needless to say.' Because when I think of Heaven I often think of the park we live next door to. One night in the middle of a particularly hot spell the summer before Caitlin was born, Weeze and I were sitting on our balcony imagining we were in New Orleans, sipping some cool fruit concoction. It was close and late and neither of us wanted to get into bed and face the hot and uncomfortable night. Without any warning, or so it seemed, the skies opened and torrential rain came flooding down from the black skies, instantly washing away the heat, the stifling humidity. It came and cleansed the world. We looked at each other for a second before making a silent pact and hand in hand we made our way downstairs, flung open the door and walked out into the warm downpour.

It was like a sensuous shower. The warm rain caressed us as we crossed over the road into the park. Our clothes became heavy and sticky and clung to our bodies. I kicked my shoes off and wandered around on the soaking carpet of grass. Weeze then took hers off and her shorts, now only covered by her long drenched shirt. I took my t-shirt off, then my trousers and finally underwear, as did Weeze, and before we knew it we were walking around a park in the middle of our town, naked and glistening in the heavy rain. It didn't really occur to us that this was inappropriate or risqué. We ran about, singing and screaming and laughing. The only light illuminating our bodies was from the occasional Victorian street lamps which are dotted around the place. Then we heard other laughter and the noise of running. We stood under a large chestnut tree and watched another young couple scurry across the path, both of them huddled under a newspaper to ward off the weather. They were giggling and hugging as they hurried along, and neither of them looked up and saw the naked couple, giggling and hugging, watching them. We lay on the ground and kissed, and the rain kept us warm and washed us clean and made us new. It was possibly the most alive, the most in love I have ever felt – it was magical and unique. It never rained like that again and we never felt as free as that again. We went back into the house, drank hot chocolate, went to bed and spooned our way to sleep. I think if I get into Heaven, I want it to be like that. I'm sure I can persuade Weeze to leave her Heaven for a little while and come and play in mine.

5 July

Sorry for the lack of news over the last few days, but I am not well. This is the first time I've staggered up to the computer since Friday. I have a new symptom, that of vomiting whenever I move around too much, so I have been flat on my back for the past few days. I feel pretty weak and dizzy. My doctor came round a couple of hours ago and liaised with Professor Gleeson and it was decided that the best plan was to get me into the hospice for a couple of days to re-hydrate me, get some anti-sickness drugs into me and hopefully get me home again, eating and drinking, by Friday. I hope so. I'm looking upon it as a free stay in a health spa – a break from the decorating here. They're going to paint our bedroom while I'm away, which will be a lovely treat to come back to – I expect I shall just sleep for a while. It's close enough for Tim and Caitlin to come and visit me and it's a new building so it should be nicer than our local NHS hospitals! I'm going to go now, as I don't feel so good, but I'll write again as soon as I can and Tim will monitor emails, I'm sure. Love you all. Au revoir.

9 July

This is just a quickie – I'm out on leave to see Caitlin in her school play *A Midsummer Night's Dream*, which was really delightful. I've sneaked home to see the decorating and get a few bits of camera equipment and the odd clean clothe. Then it's back to the hospice. I was more right than I thought when I joked about it being like a health spa – it is so tranquil and luxurious. I have an en suite bathroom, TV, video, fridge and french windows leading out into a lovely garden with pools and a waterfall.

I've stopped being sick and should be home properly on Monday. In the meantime I'm sleeping and being looked after, which is not bad once in a while. I miss Tim, of course, but it's close enough for him to come every day and I have a phone next to my bed. I feel much calmer and philosophical about things ... Our bedroom looks fabulous – all airy and light and like a sky. Tim and I are interviewing a possible nanny / mother's help tonight, then I'm back to the Hospice in the Weald.

I have been writing lists again. Things to do, to buy, to write, to everything, before ... I die. In a funny way it makes me feel very positive, as it gives me a purpose, something concrete to do ...

I wish that people with a religious message wouldn't always pick up on the sad aspects of the diary – they often say that they hear my suffering and feel the fear / pain / negative stuff – yet I don't feel that that is the main thrust of what I'm feeling / writing. I have perfectly healthy friends who seem to suffer far more half the time just through general life. This site really isn't about me asking for help from anyone / thing / entity. It is about letting people know what this is like. And this week is mostly like staring out of a window at the sky.

And so it begins. This was the beginning of the end for me. Where Weeze looked on the trip into the hospice as a break and kind of holiday, for me it was a moment of horror, a defining moment, crossing a threshold which meant really accepting death into my life. It made me sick and tearful. The whole house was in a state of disruption with the decorators beavering away, trying to get it all finished as soon as possible. The living room was wrapped in plastic and the floor was unwalkable on and our bedroom was similarly entombed. It meant that in the evening when I came home from the hospice there was nowhere for me to go, nowhere to settle. I would take Caitlin out to dinner, normally at the dreaded McDonald's, then we'd come home, I'd put her to bed and be on my own. I managed to get the telly so that it pointed out to the corridor and would sit there, my back against the radiator, until it got too late or uncomfortable and then I'd head upstairs and climb into Caitlin's bed with her. She loved this, and so did I. With Weeze gone I needed to hug Caitlin, and somehow making her know that everything was OK by hugging made me feel like perhaps that was the truth.

The hospice is fantastic and the nurses are some of the most caring and beautiful people I've come across, but I still didn't want to be there. Every day I would have to steel myself before driving the short distance to it. I could have spent a lot more time there but I just didn't want to. I didn't want to be there in that building, with a wife dying of cancer, with a child playing with toys that are put there for children with parents dying of cancer. I didn't want my wife to be in a room next to an old woman dying of cancer on one side and an old guy dying of cancer on the other. I didn't want to hear the old lady across the corridor calling out for her long dead husband as she was facing her final few days. I didn't want the guy in his mid-fifties in the first room on the ward to wink at me in a pleasant matey way every time I came in. Every day I managed to stay there for an hour or so, and then I'd pat Weeze on the hand and say something like, 'Well, OK little one, I'd better be getting off to get Caitlin ready for bed.'

The whole magnitude of the thing was just setting in around this point for me. The fact that there was a serious debate about whether or not Weeze would make it out for Caitlin's show was a real slap in the face. There was a bit of me that was just saying, 'Don't be silly, just get up and come. Come on, it's your little girl.' It takes a while for you to accept that the person you're with is really ill and I couldn't help myself feeling that Weeze was just faking it, or playing it up a bit, and that if she really wanted to she could have pulled herself together and got home earlier. In fact, these kind of mean-spirited feelings stayed with me in a very minor back-of-my-mind kind of way for a long time. They come, I think, from not wanting to accept it's really going on. There's a large part of you that just resents any bit of your life being changed, and so you end up blaming the person you love for putting you through this. With Weeze, it was when she got tired that I couldn't take it. It used to just annoy me, I think, because tiredness is an unquantifiable thing. In my head, on some level of stupidity and small-mindedness, I thought she was faking it. By which I mean I didn't want her to be not faking it.

I never ever expressed these feelings to her, and I feel mean even putting them down here, but these are the things that run through your mind. If we had to go home early from a dinner party, if I had to put Caitlin to bed for the eighth night in a row, if she just didn't want to leave the house for a walk, these were the ridiculous things that would go through my head. As she got progressively more ill, all these kind of thoughts left as there was no way she was faking throwing up or blacking out. She never faked a thing and I was just being selfish, but it takes a while to adjust.

13 July

Well, I'm back home. And what a home it is! The decorators have finished in our bedroom and it is like lying in a fairytale castle in the middle of cloud. So light and airy with the balcony doors open ... there is nowhere I'd rather be when the weather is so beautiful. Poor Tim has had a much harder week than me – he has been working flat out on the house and looking after Caitlin and things, whilst I slept and was looked after by the lovely, lovely staff at the hospice. (Thank you, you really made it a good week.)

I am now wearing an eye-patch, which has stopped me falling over! It seems the constant adjustment to my double vision was causing a lot of balance problems. Tim's brother, Jay, has got a friend who is a designer and is going to make me some glamorous designer eye-patches – we talked on the phone about velvets and beading and exotic things like that! I can't wait. I figure if you're going to wear one, there's no point in trying to hide the fact – I may as well go for it.

I'm going to write again tonight after Caitlin's asleep and copy out some of the jottings I did while I was in the hospice.

The eye-patch became an integral part of Weeze and now when I think of her I often think of her with a patch, although she in fact only wore one for five months. She wore them very well, she looked a bit like a pirate princess. I know she was worried that the patches would scare Caitlin or, worse, scare Caitlin's friends and that they'd end up making fun of her. She never wanted Caitlin to be the child with 'the funny-looking mum'. But nobody seemed to mind. She wore it with great panache and confidence and it looked as much like a fashion accessory as it did a medical aid. The difference it made to her balance was remarkable. From falling over all the time to not falling over at all in one easy step. She was back to her old self, her self-confidence returned. Like everything that had happened and was to happen, it became part of our lives.

It was just another thing, no big deal. In fact, the biggest problem was that she had always found it hard to find her glasses but now there was another thing to lose and we were forever searching round the place to find little squares of silk. I still find patches every now and then, under a sofa or tucked down the side of the bed, and I have to hold back the tears and throw them away.

14 July

Well, I didn't get around to writing again last night, and it's afternoon today already. I basically feel like crap in the mornings at the moment, so the day doesn't really start for me until about two.

The house is looking great as Toni (Tim's mum) came down and did a good solid day's cleaning. My mum has been working hard too – mess is something tangible to get angry with and do something about, I think.

The hospice re-focused me on Stuff To Do Before I Die – which is about where this diary came in, back in February, I think.

Letters. Letters are very important to me. Whilst I was in the hospice I re-watched one of my all-time favourite films – *Cyrano de Bergerac*. Love letter – infinitely more meaningful than any other form of communication. I am going to buy a load of wonderful paper and sealing wax – the letters that I am writing now are meant to be kept . . .

My other favourite film is *Babette's Feast* and I watched that last week too. It's about a woman who blows everything on one marvellous, extravagant gesture . . . I would urge everyone to see it. My one eye held up all right for the subtitles, too.

I spent a whole afternoon looking at the sunlight playing on my feet and felt sad that I don't have time to go and study art and light and photography ... then it occurred to me that I was so fortunate really – people have lifetimes without discovering a passion for anything, without seeing the wonder that is all around us – here was I, able to see the beauty of light and with the leisure to revel in it!

A little thing I wrote:

She dragged my father in from the playroom across the hall and handed me a picture.

'It's a moon-sausage balloon,' she announced in the manner of one who knows how good her work is and needs no praise. 'Show her yours, Paul,' she commanded.

My father put his picture on the end of the bed. Caitlin felt it needed some explanation.

'His is a man looking over a wall.'

I looked up at my lovely, sweet father.

'It's not finished,' he said.

15 July

I'm finally feeling on top of things a bit. Since I came home we've sorted out cleaning and Caitlin's help so that we're now pretty much covered for the house and me not being on my own. Tim's going out to see some comedy in London tonight, which will be a great break for him – I don't want his life to be only looking after me and Caitlin – he needs to do fun stuff too. Of course being with me is fun, but you know what I mean.

I'm in a blowing money mood. Luxury is my middle name at the moment. I spent most of my life saving things for special occasions – I think we all do. We don't wear our really good

clothes, the ones that make you look and feel fabulous –
because we're saving them for more important days. We
don't eat with the silver, because it's just for dinner parties.
Well, I've really discovered what the phrase 'life is not a
rehearsal' is about. It's about living as though every day is the
grand occasion. If you have or can afford wonderful things,
use them. They make you feel good. I bought a multi-layered
floaty chiffon nightdress to go with our airy new bedroom
and I feel so glamorous. If I'm bedridden I want to receive
people looking beautiful.

I've noticed that my diary is reflecting a very vain person
at the moment – I think that vanity is one of those things,
like anger, that one can spend a lot of time thinking is a 'bad'
feeling and a selfish one. Now that I'm less inhibited about
everything I can admit to myself and to the world that I
LIKE BEAUTIFUL THIINGS. I LIKE WEARING BEAUTIFUL
EXPENSIVE CLOTHES AND I LIKE TO BE IN A BEAUTIFUL
HOUSE, MY PLACE, AN EXTENSION OF ME AND TIM
AND CAITLIN.

Louise grew up in a privileged family where money was
never really a problem. Sure, they occasionally got broke,
but never in the same way that other families do. There
was always family money to bail them out. From the age
of eighteen Weeze came into an inheritance and was given
a healthy monthly income to live off. She was very torn
over the whole issue – she felt she had never done anything to deserve the money and so wasn't really sure she
was comfortable having it. What made it even more difficult was that her two adopted sisters, Dee and Jan, whom
she thought of as being as much her sisters as her blood
sister Anthea, were not entitled to any of it, it was a pure

blood inheritance. For all her guilt though, she loved what it gave her: the freedom to do what she wanted, a nice house to live in, regular meals out, nice clothes and generally a life devoid of penny pinching. But the curse of it was that she found it difficult in her early life to find a motivation or a purpose. She wasn't driven by the need to earn a living, she was driven by a need to find out who she was. And that's a scary thing. If you're given the world and someone says go on, do whatever you want, what do you do?

She went through lots of things: aromatherapy, reflexology, acupuncture, Buddhism, Taoism, vegetarianism, colour therapy, T'ai Chi, Chi Gun, cheffing, making chutneys, mosaicing, dyeing her hair, being a hippy, smoking pot, playing saxophone. And a million and one other things. She had a natural aptitude for most things she turned her hand to which meant that very little was a challenge to her. Within a few weeks she could be proficient at nearly anything – sickening really. But because of this, she rarely went on to become great at something, there was no challenge for her. She also never had to stick at anything for financial reasons. Cancer put her whole life into focus. Life wasn't something to be taken for granted, there wasn't always going to be a tomorrow to do things. And in the five years or so she had cancer she became incredibly focused and creative and, weirdly enough, disciplined.

There is nothing in here that Weeze wouldn't have owned up to herself. What was really sad is that the one thing she truly discovered to be her talent and her passion, photography, was something that took time to develop and find a voice in. And she did this. She knew what she did well and it was capture people, capture their essence, and had she been given another five years I'm sure that her body of work would have been outstanding.

It should be said that she was never a rich woman, not *rich* rich, but she had enough to make life easier and she would regularly say that she wouldn't know how she'd cope with the cancer if she was in different circumstances. If she'd been in a tiny flat in a high-rise block living hand to mouth, the cancer, on top of everything else, would have driven her round the bend. When she was well, able to go out and indulge in some retail therapy, then having money was a big, big bonus. But when she was really ill towards the end, there was nothing all the money in the world could have done. That's when you find out the real power of money and it truly is an impotent thing.

16 July

No kidding I was in a blowing money mood. I bought ... a digital camera!!! Tim persuaded me, not that I needed much persuading, and I got a Sony 950. It has a viewing screen at the back so I don't have to look through a viewfinder – big advantage for ol' one eye here – and has manual settings, does black and white and is generally fantastic. It can also be angled around so I can take self-portraits properly and see the viewing screen while I'm doing them. The other big advantage is that I can stick them up on here really quickly without having to have them processed, scanned, etc. I got it last night and had a play for a tiny bit, then was sick all day today, so haven't had a chance to do too much yet, but by next week there should be pictures of the new house decorations and me up on here . . .

The being sick all day thing was totally my own fault, as I

forgot to take my sickness pill last night. Made me realize quite how at the mercy of the drugs I am at the moment – still, they enable me to be upright when I remember to take them. Tim and Caitlin have been doing lots of cooking since I went into the hospice. A few days ago they made some excellent 'Wallace and Gromit' shaped cookies, which came out really well.

Today they made fudge, which went less well. Caitlin sat on my bed this evening and said, 'Daddy and I made fudge and it was supposed to be vanilla fudge but it burnt so much it looked like chocolate fudge.'

She put her hand in front of her mouth and whispered, 'Daddy had to throw the saucepan away.'

I think it's so sweet, them learning to do things together. It helps me because I can see through things like that that they will be OK. Things will occasionally go wrong, but they will laugh about mistakes and learn and go on. Caitlin sometimes gives Tim a big squeeze and says, 'Mummy's getting iller, but we're getting stronger, aren't we, Daddy?' I see that as a recognition that their relationship is getting stronger as a unit of two and that comforts me. The stronger they are, the less either of them will go to pieces when I die.

Now fudge is a lot harder than you'd think and the recipe in the book was entirely misleading! You get all this sugar, put it in a saucepan and then have to bring it up to this specific heat, and that's about all it says. It doesn't tell you how to bring it up to this heat or that if the substance turns black and becomes a solid block then you've gone severely wrong. It also doesn't say that should you make these mistakes, the resulting mess will be welded on to your expensive Le Creuset saucepan and that no amount of scrubbing, boiling or anything, in fact, will remove the so-called toffee. What I have discovered, however, is that they do make excellent flower pots!

As you can probably tell, I'm not the world's best chef. Caitlin and I are currently on a voyage of discovery. 'Does this go with this, Caitlin?' Scrumpled up face and a 'yurrrgh!' mean no. 'Does this go with this?' Pensive look then broad smile and giggles mean yes. Quite simple really. This week I've made pilchard pie, some excellent pork burgers and umpteen pasta dishes. Caitlin, on the other hand, spent all of yesterday making a potion of some of the nastiest stuff she could find at the back of our cupboards. When I asked what the grim mess was for, she winked at me and said, 'It's a love potion, it makes people fall in love with you.' When I asked her who she was going to use it on she said, 'You Daddy, of course.' I told her that she didn't need a potion for that as I loved her more than anything in the whole world already. She looked quizzically around for a minute and then said, 'OK, it's a transforming potion, it transforms people into animals, does that sound good?' It did sound good but we're still not sure how effective it is as we can't get any person to come within three yards of it, let alone take a sip.

17 July

A better day today – I watched *Star Wars* (the first one) on video with Caitlin this morning. Then she went and played at my parents whilst I got to grips a bit more with the digital camera – very exciting stuff. I joined Caitlin for dinner and we played Star Wars lots – she was R2D2 and spent the evening communicating in bleeps.

News from my parents was that my cousin Kate has just had a baby girl. We have had a couple of births around us recently and they are a good reminder of the cycle of life, and how it is not wrong that there is death because there is also birth. And birth is so wonderful. We hope to get down to Devon to see the baby soon.

It is a lovely evening tonight and we have loads of night-scented honeysuckle by our front door. I can just sit on the balcony leading out from our bedroom and breathe . . . I feel very peaceful tonight. Earlier I was worrying about my time – wanting to do camera stuff and letters and lots of people ringing up to come round and . . . now I feel very calm. It will all work itself out and things will either happen or not. People are very understanding about my cancelling things if I feel like. I trust fate – I will have the right amount of time.

19 July

Yippee! Back to my old self . . . well, my self of a month or so ago. Pre-hospice, anyway. I had a most productive day. I organized and cleared out my desk and its drawers of paper things – theatre tickets, free postcards from racks in the cinema, phone numbers of long-forgotten relevance, urgently underlined messages on the backs of bank statements and every single picture Caitlin has ever done (most undated, of course).

I felt hugely lighter and more in control when I had done it – as though I now have the necessary clarity to write those letters. I put all the phone numbers Tim needs to ring when I actually die together – you know, cheerful stuff like that. I have decided I can possibly delay actually dying by having so much to do that I can keep Death on hold, saying, 'I'm perfectly happy to die, but please wait until I've finished this . . .' I've already got an infinite number of 'this's'.

The other big and terribly exciting news today is that my darling mother has got Tim and me a balloon flight! I've been saying I wanted one for a while, and she knew we'd take ages to get round to it, so she went and did it, whilst I'm feeling well. It's on Tuesday evening (a week tomorrow) or Wednesday if the weather's no good on Tues. I CANNOT WAIT.

20 July

This morning I went to an indoor play place called 'Wear'M'Out' with Caitlin and a friend of mine plus children. It was utterly exhausting. Even though all I did was sit and have a coffee, just being surrounded by so many children knocked me out. Almost literally, actually, as I pushed Caitlin on a swing for a couple of minutes and didn't judge the distance properly, due to my eye-patch, and the swing crashed into my right cheekbone, which was most painful. Still, you live and learn.

When I came home, Helen, who is helping us out with Caitlin, etc., took said child off to her house for the afternoon, so I sat down to do some paperwork. I had no sooner started a list of 'important memory things for Caitlin to be put in a box – hopefully made by me', when I felt suddenly crushingly tired. I could feel my energy leaching out of me. A combination of being worn out by the morning and the emotional exhaus- tion of the task in hand. So I went to bed and didn't wake up until half-past five, when Caitlin returned. In this weather siestas feel normal.

When I have no responsibilities, my natural state is stay up late and sleep in the afternoons, I think. And now that I'm lucky enough to have so many people helping me do what I like, I'm reverting to it. It reminds me of my early teens when I lived in Athens: a life spent (mis-spent, some would say), dedicated to fun with no thought for the future.

Youth, in other words.

22 July

Ill again yesterday – in bed and asleep all day. I'm beginning to realize that I am possibly not going to get a great deal better than this. 'This' being one day in bed for every three or so that I'm up. And by 'up' I don't mean running marathons or anything, I literally mean up.

I went into the sitting-room on Tuesday evening and Tim and Caitlin were watching *Return of the Jedi* and having such fun, so excited, so cuddly and loving. I decided to re-prioritize a bit. All the lists of numbers, the organization of our finances and paperwork and things that I have been attempting to find the energy for – they aren't important. Tim will sort it all out later and people will rally round and help him. What is important is having quality time with Tim and Caitlin. This website is important too – I had no idea when I started it that it would become quite so important to me, but it is. It's my big stab at immortality, it's one of the things that makes me feel that not all of me will leave this Earth. That I can make an impact, however small, on people's lives. It is also my therapy.

Time feels as though it is sliding through my fingers like oil at the moment – and sleep beckons almost all the time. But I am not ready yet.

Over the last few days I have been trying to sort out my birthday celebrations. Convinced that it will be the last birthday I will be in a fit state to party, I was frequently to be seen amid a pile of brochures and diaries, comparing the dates that various of my family could do, and the numerous venues that offered spit roast pigs, sit-down meals, accommodation for sixty ... Yesterday I had a huge panic dream about it all and woke up more stressed than when I went to sleep. Tim also reminded me how exhausting our wedding was and how, when you have a party of more than fifty, you don't actually get to talk to anyone anyway. So. No big party. And oh, the relief. Perhaps I shall be 'At Home', as they used to say, for a few days to receive visitors, but I'm not going to organize much.

My elder sister Dee and her husband George have been staying for the last couple of days and it's been lovely. I have stayed up late and talked lots and (as yet) not had to pay for it – I feel great. Except for the pain in my throat and the back of my tongue, which has increased somewhat. We went out to dinner with Dee, George and my parents last night and sat around outside. I had my first glass of wine in ages and it was so relaxing – like being on holiday. With the house almost finished and looking beautiful, this is how I want my life to be – surrounded by people I love, talking and laughing over good food in a lovely environment. (The weather has improved again, you may note, and with it my mood.) When my laptop computer being mended situation is sorted out, and I can write from bed again, my life will be pretty damn good.

During the summer months Weeze loved to be outside as much as she could. Before her radiotherapy her favourite part of the day was when the sun was at its height, beating the earth, scorching everything. She loved to lie in it and soak it up. Often, when it was far too hot for a pale-skinned youth like me, she would lie there, serene and blissed out. However, the radiotherapy really effected her love of the sun. The skin on her face never really recovered fully and was always very sensitive – any hot sunlight on it was painful. She did try occasionally to relive her years in the sun by lying in the back garden with a silk scarf over her face, whilst the rest of her semi-naked form bathed in the light. But this was unsatisfactory and she never lasted out in it very long. So she then came to love early evening in the garden when the sting of heat had passed. She'd make these giant Greek salads, dripping with olive oil, set up a table on the patio and sit there drinking wine and reading into the night. At around eight o'clock the sun dips over the horizon and casts long shadows all over the next-door park. It also cast a perfect shadow on to our painted outhouse wall of us dining. It was like having guests – we would raise a glass, they would raise a glass, one of us would leave to go inside to get more wine and so one of our ghost partners would also depart for more refreshments.

On a particularly warm, exquisite night, my father grabbed some of Caitlin's purple pavement chalks and sketched round the shadow party, capturing a moment, a feeling of joy. It stayed there for the whole summer and then slowly, as autumn encroached on our lives and the rain came, it was washed off, streaking its way down into the earth below.

26 July

I found some writing I did in Guy's when I was pretty ill the first time, three years ago.

> Morphine
> Morphine.
> Like an injection of ink into water.
> Clouds of morphia,
> Billowing into my body
> Soft and beguiling,
> Obscuring my pain
> And with it, my mind.
> Morphine.
> Like waves lapping a sandy shore.
> Little crests of morphine
> Breaking over my body,
> Promising to cleanse.
> Washing me of pain
> My thoughts drift out to sea.
> Morphine.
> Like a lullaby for a miserable child,
> Soft syllables of morphus
> Drifting into my senses
> Hypnotizing, soothing,
> Singing away my pain
> And rocking to sleep my brain.

You know you've got cancer when they finally give you morphine. I find the word strangely fascinating. Mor-phine. My tongue lingers over it. It reminds me of the last century – people dulling their pain with it, becoming addicts, having to use more and more. The word is syrupy, like the sticky contents of tinted bottles with glass stoppers, kept high up on the back shelf in a musty old chemist's shop. The word laudanum has a similar, almost romantic property for me. After all, they are both opiates. Derivatives from the poppy fields of the mystical East. Sherlock Holmes and all that.

As I lie in my cleanly starched hospital bed in Guy's, I imagine myself transported from this white, neon-lit ward, back to the London of a hundred years ago. I am below street level in a land of whores and rascals. An opium den. The atmosphere is thick and musty – much like my brain in its present condition – and faceless forms droop from the edges of rudimentary bunks. They murmur and shriek from their fantasies, existing in another place, another time. Like me, they have escaped.

I wander about the ward, half in the here and now, half in my opium den, and regard the crew of miscreants I am surrounded by. What have they done or been to bring them here on their journey through life?

Apparently lorry drivers make up one of the largest single professions represented here. Now why should that be? What karmic problems are inherent in the driving of goods across our Earth? If the answer is pollution and the depletion of the ozone layer, it seems a bit harsh to me . . . The doctors tell me it is the unhealthy food, smoking and the sedentary lifestyle. It's probably true, but then why am I here?

My hair hasn't fallen out from the chemotherapy. I rather hoped that I would at least lose it from my legs and armpits. No such luck.

My thoughts are random and balloon-like, floating and bobbing cheerfully along from one topic to another. As I told the nurse, the morphine hasn't completely stopped the pain, but it has made me care less about it. I am no longer focused on the all-encompassing soreness of my mouth which, like an image close to the lens, obliterated all sense of perspective. There was only pain. Now the pain is just another cloudy object in the sky that my mind occasionally bobs past.

When I was a child I learnt French from a book called *Le Ballon Rouge* and that is how my mind seems to me now, a small red balloon, floating about, detached from the world, unanchored by string. 'When I was a child.' I feel scarcely more than a child now, and yet I have one of my own. It's astounding. Do we ever understand anything? Or do we just bob along doing whatever comes next? Millions of little balloons simply turning the pages of their lives. Not that I have any great desire to understand anything at the moment. I just wondered.

Three years on, morphine is considerably less romantic, but I think the writing holds up.

I remember really clearly going into the chemo ward at Guy's the day that she'd first had morphine. The night before, she'd been in a real state, the radiotherapy had pretty much destroyed her tongue and she found swallowing anything agonizing. The chemotherapy made her feel poisoned and sick. She'd held my hand and garbled as best she could through the pain about how miserable she felt and begged me to take her home.

'It's just poison,' she said, pointing to the bag of chemicals slowly being leaked into her body.

She was in real agony with it all, and I couldn't stand it. I told her we'd wait one more night and if it was still as bad then I'd take her away from it all. That night things got worse and they gave her a morphine driver, a little syringe on a machine that she could control – one push of a button and she'd get a fresh dose of bliss. As I walked down the ward towards her I could see the difference from twenty yards. Her face was relaxed and she was smiling.

'You look better.'

'You bet I do,' she giggled and tapped the box at her side.

I had no idea that these syringe drivers would become a significant part of my life in the last months of Weeze's life. If they were up and running things were OK. If they broke down, ran out of batteries or got clogged up, life would be hell until they were fixed. There is nothing quite like the relief that comes with seeing someone you love in pain and then watching that pain go, drift away from them.

Weeze had real trouble getting through the whole chemo experience and more than once I would arrive and find her in tears. I'd sit there for a couple of hours giving her a pep talk, reminding her why she was doing it. By the time I left she had just about enough courage to get her through to our next chat the next day, when we'd go through it all again. It was the only bit of her treatment that I think she regretted. She was never really convinced that it had any beneficial effect, but who knows? If it only extended her life by a week, it's another week I'm grateful for.

27 July

Well, the balloon didn't fly – too much wind. Perhaps tomorrow instead. I took some self-portraits this morning and hopefully there will be a new picture of me on the home page here VERY SOON. I'm still waiting for my laptop computer to be fixed – in the meantime I'm working off Tim's and have to fight him for time when he's not writing his novel! His novel is BRILLIANT, by the way. Very funny. And he's written a third of it so far, so it's coming along really well.

My birthday plans are now a big evening picnic on the beach, which will be great if the weather is nice. Good and informal, anyway. My only concern now is that the day will become overloaded with meaning ('Will it be the last birthday the poor girl will ever see?') I want it to just be fun. In the meantime I've asked Tim to get me some extra lenses for my digital camera, which I'm discovering is VERY COOL.

If I only achieve one thing for Weeze in the future it's to finish this stupid novel thing I've been doing for years. Every year since I was eighteen I've tried to write a novel, a different novel each year, not the same one – that would be too sad. I always get right near the end, then I stop. It drives me crazy and it used to drive Weeze bananas too. She would read my output each day, get really excited, be desperate to know what happened at the end and then I'd miss a couple of days with a cold, or decide I'd done so well I'd take a holiday from it, and before you knew it, it was filed in my drawer called 'Novels – bugger'. To keep her happy, I'd always tell her what happened at the end of the story and I think this was a problem as well – once I'd told Weeze the story, I felt I didn't have to tell anyone else. It was done. The person who I was writing it for already knew the story, so why bother finishing it. But I make this vow to everyone, I will finish the one I'm working on, 'Meacham and Building Number 5'. It may never get published, but that was never really what it was about.

━━

Weeze just wanted me to finish one of the damn things. I didn't tell Weeze the end of it, so I feel that by writing the ending down she'll somehow find it out. Never fear, Weeze, we will find out what happens to the snail star chart and the talking cat.

28 July

A guest book entry I got today highlighted something I've been mulling over for a while. That is, the integrity of this site as a diary, given that I know lots of people read it and they also interact with me. So. Can I keep this diary honest, or do I write with an audience in mind?

The diaries I wrote when I was thirteen and on up all contain a measure of self-consciousness – I have always enjoyed reading published diaries and I think that lurking in the subconscious of most diarists there is a dream that they might one day be published. That said, I think if I were to lie on these pages it would negate the whole point. Which is . . . I don't know. It is certainly therapy – after all, people pay therapists to just listen. When I started it I had no idea I would get the kind of response I'm getting. The thought that it is helping people understand this process and that it is used by hospice staff as a counselling tool, just blows me away and makes me feel some good is coming of all this. I do occasionally feel I 'ought' to write something – the last time that happened I put in all the morphine stuff. Rather than write stuff I didn't feel at the time I thought I would copy out some older stuff that I wanted to put in some time anyway.

The site has become immensely important to me, though. It is what I do. I want everyone to be on the web, so I can show all the people I know what I'm doing. Most of our friends aren't on the Net and so have never read it. My mother is a little worried that I'll get a big head because of all the lovely things people say in the guest book. And maybe I do engineer that a little. After all, this is only what I choose to write – so I guess it must be a bit censored. But not very. I'm generally thinking straight on to the screen – typing as I think. I do miss out stuff about other people sometimes if I don't think they'd like me putting it in – after all, my family aren't doing this, I am, so I don't think I have the right to quote them too much.

Mostly it helps me to know I'm making some positive impact on the world before I die. I think that's how everyone would like to be remembered.

29 July

An embarrassing thing happened the other day. Caitlin was out having lunch at someone's house and so I was taking some pictures – amongst others, the self-portrait on the home page. Anyway, one of the joys of a digital camera is that you don't get the pictures developed . . . so I was doing some, shall we say, rather risqué pictures, when Tim walked in. Well, one thing led to another and . . . and I forgot to tell you that the paint on the front door was drying, so it was wide open. As was every other door in the house. So. When the deed was done, the phone rang. Tim got up to answer it and happened to look out of the window, to see my mother's car reversing out of our road at great speed.

When I phoned her up later she at first tried to save us by denying it, but then gave in. I reminded her that I had walked in on them a few times in my youth.

'We forgot the front door was open,' I said.

'Yes,' she replied. 'All the doors were open.'

Which probably means she came right into the bedroom. Still at least she (and now you) know that we don't spend all our time doing cancer stuff.

What's strange about this entry isn't that we'd been caught by Smo having sex, it's rather the fact that we'd never been caught before. When I think of Weeze, I think of sex. That was a very large part of our relationship, as big a part as any other aspect of it. I think both of us really blossomed sexually throughout our relationship. Although I was never sure that she was telling the truth or whether she was just massaging my ego, she always claimed that she had hardly had orgasms before with her previous boyfriends. Now, I'm sure every woman reading this is probably thinking, 'Yeah, how many times have I said that. Poor deluded fool, did he really fall for that?' And possibly the boyfriends she was talking about might remember things differently, but I do think we had something really special. It was everything – it was tender, dirty, beautiful, filthy, spiritual and base. And it got better and better. As we learnt what each other liked, as we explored each other's imaginations, we kept finding new levels. I don't think if there were marks given for sexual performance I'd score terribly high on a chart rating moves, size, sensitivity or ingenuity. But with Weeze I was a great lover, a Valentino or an Errol Flynn, and it was all to do with her. She had no hang-ups or inhibitions, she was as sexually free a person as I've ever met. She was also a talker, she knew what she wanted and what she didn't want and would ask or tell or beg for me to do it. And satisfying her made me feel unbelievably fulfilled and whole and calm. And when we had sex I would fall in love with her all over again – the touch of her soft skin, the heat she radiated, entrapped me in desire.

I remember so clearly the first time I saw her undressed, I mean really saw her. We'd made love the night before, but in the dark, and then both scurried quickly into dressing-gowns the next morning. But the following night I came over to the house, she cooked me the most amazing light meal, we ate and she disappeared upstairs.

'Tim, come up here, I want you to see something.'

I climbed the stairs two at a time and there, standing at the end of the corridor in the bedroom doorway, was Louise. Dressed in black lace bra and panties, stockings, suspenders and red high heels. She was motioning me towards her. I just couldn't believe how sexy she looked. Her body was exquisite, toned, tanned. The shock was partly because I'd never realized that a body like that was hidden beneath all her floaty, hippy clothes. This was a revelation, a minor epiphany. For the first time in my life I was in awe of someone's naked body. I looked up at her long long legs, over her stomach, her perfect breasts, up to her smiling face, and was in awe. It was all too much. I began to laugh and just turned around and walked away. It took me about ten minutes of giggling and inching towards her before I could actually get close enough to feel her skin against mine. She loved it, she loved the power she felt, the fact that through my reactions for that moment she was the most beautiful woman in the world. And she was to me.

Louise was very much a summer person, she loved the heat of the sun on her body and could sit in our hammock on our balcony all day just reading and soaking up the rays. She was like a cat – the sun made her body fluid, slinky. I loved coming home after she had been lying in the sun all day. I'd come out on to the balcony, give her a long cold drink, which she'd sip, and then she'd grab my hand, pull me inside and wrap me in the warmth. Her skin would soak up the sun – you could smell it on her, smell the heat, the joy, the relaxation it gave her. It was unbelievably sexy.

I can remember the night we got pregnant with Caitlin – or if it wasn't then it was very close to that. We made love in front of the fire on the sofa, and it was one of those joining with your partner, really making love, kind of sessions, as opposed to the sex, do-it-to-me-now kind. We spent a lot of time during sex just holding each other while I was inside her, kissing gently, not moving a lot, just enjoying the sensation of touching the other's body. I can still feel her on me if I close my eyes. It's like my body, my skin, remembers the feeling. I can remember every inch of her body, kissing every bit of her. I worshipped her body. When we made love, I got lost in her, overwhelmed by the beauty that she was. Every part of her body was exquisite to me – the soft skin of the inside bit of her elbow, what is that bit called? The velvet skin of her inside thigh, which would make her buck uncontrollably. The fact that her ears were too sensitive, so much so that you couldn't go near them. If you timed it just right and kissed them just as she achieved orgasm she'd go crazy with desire, but a second either way and you could blow the whole thing.

Anyway, on this particular night we'd made love for what seemed like for ever (but then, doesn't it always for men? – just thought I'd get that in before anyone else does) when Louise asked me to stop.

'Please, please stop, I can't take it any more, it's too

much, my head's gone funny. I can't cum again, I'm dizzy, my head's just gone.'

Now these are the kind of things that every man dreams of hearing, but are precisely the kind of things which are least likely to make him stop. So we kept on going.

'Please, please, Tim, it's too much, I can't think straight.' She then began to laugh loads. 'Christ, stop it, I can actually see stars. It's all sparkling. I love you. You made me see stars.'

Well, what more could you want? We spent the next week gagging with each other about how good I was in bed, so good in fact that I'd made her see stars. To say I felt ridiculously proud would have been an understatement – for the briefest time I went round thinking I was the greatest lover in the world. It later turned out that she had actually seen stars, or rather sparkling lights. It was a symptom of her illness. As the tumour grew it pressed on her optic nerve and caused her to quite often lose her sight, seeing only sparkling lights. Still, it makes a good story – I made someone so aroused she actually saw stars.

While we're talking about sex and what a goer Weeze was, let me tell you about just after we found out she had cancer for the first time. She'd kill me if she knew I was going to spill the beans about this, but it sums up a lot of Weeze for me. And it'll make me laugh to write it down so – sorry, Weeze.

We'd only just had Caitlin when we got the news of the cancer and, what with one thing and another, we hadn't left Caitlin for the night and hadn't gone out on our own for an evening. Weeze thought we could do with a night out so she arranged a surprise for me. Smo came over and Weeze said, 'Right, Tim we're going out, we need a night to ourselves. I've organized everything. Get your coat, we're off.'

I was probably more nervous about leaving Caitlin than Weeze was, and wasn't sure I was ready to leave her – what a soppy git. But this wasn't helped by the fact that as we made our way towards the front door, Smo coming down the stairs to say goodbye tripped and in slow-motion fell headfirst, with my tiny baby in her hands. She managed to spin herself around so that when she actually hit the stairs it was her back and not Caitlin that took the full brunt of the impact. She then slid at great speed down the remaining stairs before coming to rest in a heap at our feet with Caitlin's head just centimetres from the iron radiator. How she or Caitlin weren't hurt I'll never know, but for some reason it shattered my confidence about leaving her. Smo was so full of apologies and so desperate not to ruin the night that I found myself leaving the house in spite of myself. Weeze and I sat in the car outside the house for about half an hour, telling each other it was fine and that it could have happened to anyone, and that it would be too terrible for Smo if we were to go back in and say we didn't trust her with Caitlin. Besides, Weeze explained that she had gone to quite a lot of effort and that we should really go out.

As we drove through Tunbridge Wells she began to give me clues as to what we were up to. We drove towards a hotel I knew really well, as an ex-girlfriend of mine had worked there. I knew everyone in the entire place. When it became obvious we were heading for the Royal Wells, I naïvely said, 'Oh, dinner at the Wells, that'll be great, really relaxing. I love the Wells.'

Louise looked somewhat surprised.

'You mean you know the Wells?'

I explained about my history with the place. We got out of the car and, instead of heading for the restaurant, Louise headed for the reception. About five members of staff winked at me, nudged me and said hi. As Weeze was signing the register she informed me that she'd booked a room for a couple of hours. She couldn't have booked it for the whole night, oh no, just for a quickie, was how she described it to the girl at the desk when she'd booked it. I was about as embarrassed as I've ever been. The man who led us up to our room chatted away with me about old times and I tried to drop in as many times as possible that Louise was my wife and this was perfectly acceptable behaviour with one's wife.

'How was I to know you'd know everyone?'

'Of all the places though. I don't know whether I can do it tonight, here of all places, and what with Smo falling down the stairs I'm just not sure I feel like a night of passion.'

Weeze smiled. 'Oh really, well, I tell you what, you lie on the bed and watch some telly. I'll just pop into the bathroom and we'll see how the night goes, huh?'

She came out ten minutes later dressed in a full policewoman's outfit complete with handcuffs and a video camera and an ominous-looking bag of stuff. My resolve managed to hold out about half a millisecond and two hours later we were heading back to the car exhausted. Louise had a massive Cheshire cat's smile on her face as she settled the bill, and I looked stunned and shell-shocked. When we got home Smo said, 'Good night?'

'Great night,' was all Weeze said.

I said nothing, still gobsmacked by my wife. And that was why sex stayed great right up until the end – it never got dull or run of the mill, one or other of us could always find something to do which surprised and excited the other. Cool, huh?

31 July

This is probably going to sound hugely egotistical and possibly even mad, but here goes . . .

In bed last night I realized with a sudden clarity why I don't want to go to spiritual healers or try any weird cures. It is because I feel that this is my destiny, for want of a better word. When I started doing this website it felt, for the first time in my life, as though I had discovered what it is I was born to do. And I think that the fulfilment of this destiny culminates in my death. The thing that makes it meaningful is that I am talking about it – my job, if you like, is to talk about death and to de-mystify it as it is happening to me. I feel as though I am participating in a process that will end in death, not in some miraculous healing, and that the value of the experience is showing the world that death is not so terrible. That death is inevitable and that therefore we would all be a lot better off if we could accept that death is an integral part of the experience of life.

End of sermon.

Chapter 8

―――

2 August

That last entry sounded so definite and assertive, didn't it? 'It is my destiny . . .' I do think it, but I know that it is also my way of making sense of this situation. In the same way that religious types think 'I'm scared of death, but if I say this is God's plan and there is a reason for all this, then it makes dying easier.' Then again, that could be used to explain away all of man's beliefs. They are explanations created to help us make sense of the world.

Tim and I want to buy a flat in Brighton. It may sound like a crazy time to be doing it, but bear with me.

1. We love decorating places, and to have a little studio flat to play with would be excellent fun.

2. To give us a holiday home half an hour's drive away – somewhere to escape and sit on the beach.

3. To give Tim options after I'm dead. This is the main reason, really. He may not want to stay in Tunbridge Wells surrounded by people we knew as a couple. He may get pissed off with everyone keeping an eye on him to see how he's doing. He may want a new start with Caitlin. This way he can get to know a few people there now, as well as schools and things. Or he could let it to students and use it as an investment.

This house is so much me, I can't imagine him being able to bring a girl back here! Whereas somewhere we've never really lived together could be a good place for Tim and Caitlin to start again. Incidentally, the rules are: six months deep mourning with no looking at another girl. Then a one-night stand he feels awful about. Then after a year he can start looking at girls he likes. I'm going to try to load this now – new months are a bit tricky.

Mmm, well . . . Almost directly after Weeze died I got the biggest rush of sexual desire I can remember in my life. In the middle of my grief there was this passion, this urge to be with someone, to have sex with someone. It racked me with guilt, but it was undeniable. It was something about grabbing life. Wanting to know that I was still alive, that my life hadn't ended with the death of my wife. I also wanted to know that I was still attractive, that I hadn't been marked or scarred by the whole thing. I had this feeling that all the experiences were there in my eyes, on my face, and that this would be me for ever, the shell me, the husk of what I was. I wanted someone to show me in a physical way that that wasn't true, that I could still be alive, even when so much of my life had been living in death. It gradually waned – well, a little bit anyway. Now I don't know how I feel, just tired I guess.

3 August

It is 1 a.m. We've just had dinner with some lovely friends — luckily ones I feel very relaxed with — and I cried in front of someone other than Tim for the first time in years, as far as I can remember. I was putting Caitlin to bed and she was taking ages and being really difficult, when she suddenly said, 'I'm really cross with your cancer, Mummy . . . I think everyone is cross with your cancer.' Then, later on, 'Let's talk about something else, Mummy. I don't want to worry about your cancer.'

It just seemed to hit me and I felt like I couldn't breathe. I took her downstairs to have dinner with us and watch a video or something, because I knew otherwise I would just cry and squeeze her too hard. As it was, I cried a little with our friends. Caitlin seemed to be very matter of fact: when she said she didn't want to talk about it, she didn't. I felt like it came totally out of left field. I think because we were trying to have a grown-up dinner party, it made it harder for me — it was as though it was a reminder that I am not / cannot lead a 'normal' life. Because it was the first time this has really come up, I just wanted to give in and let her stay up until 11.30 and eat ice cream in front of the telly. We're all learning together and I guess we'll feel our way as we go. At least we're talking about it with her.

Later

At lunchtime today I was given the most wonderful children's-type birthday party by the same people who came to dinner last night. I nearly cried in front of them again, it was so lovely. They had made me a savoury birthday cake because I can't eat sweet stuff. It was a house made of smoked salmon sandwiches and decorated with cream cheese and Twiglets and roof tiles made of little crackers. They went to so much trouble. The children all referred to me as 'birthday girl'. I felt utterly spoilt in a lovely way – it was like I was a child again and I was really special. As an adult and a mother I don't think you can feel that very often. Tim, meanwhile, has been hopping around the house for the last couple of days, barely able to conceal his excitement about the treats he has planned for me. He says I have forty-eight hours of treats from 11 a.m. tomorrow morning. I am so lucky.

Today in general I have felt pretty exhausted, but I think it has to do with last night in that it was emotionally tiring. As I've said before, there is a world of difference between dealing with something on a philosophical level and dealing with it in reality out of the blue. Last night I had had a glass of champagne (about my limit mixed with the morphine) and a houseful of dinner party friends and didn't feel ready to talk to Caitlin about it all. I suppose it's just that it's the first time she's initiated a conversation about the cancer. Plus, of course, no one is ever really ready for much of what life throws at them: life is about dealing with what you're given. Catching the curve balls. I have no idea if that makes sense – catching the curve balls, I mean. I know nothing about baseball that can't be learnt from watching *Field of Dreams*. If any of my American audience wish to correct me, please feel free. Right, it's hot, I'm babbling and I want to be well-rested for tomorrow (and Thursday), so farewell, my friends, until we speak again.

5 August

Well. What a birthday. I fear that if I live to see the next one, several people will be asking for their money back, so over-the-top has this year been! On Wednesday I got some presents and then went down to the only sandy beach here-abouts for a surprise birthday picnic. Lots of running about on the sand in lovely warm wind and paddling, surrounded by people I love. It was beautiful and emotional.

Then, yesterday ... WOW. A limo picked Tim and me up here at 11 a.m. We then went to the Criterion restaurant (chef: Marco Pierre White) for lunch. Then on to Harrods for a massage and manicure, then Harvey Nicks for 'personal shopping', then Quo Vadis (Marco's other restaurant) for dinner, then the show *Copenhagen*, then home. The limo taking us between stops and home, of course. It was all dreamy film-star stuff, but highlights for me were:

The food – he's the only chef I know where you can really order anything – even stuff you think you'll hate – and you will love it. Then there's the personal shopping! The assistant gets all the stuff you want in your size for you, so I just had to do a fashion show for Tim (and George, who was in London and dropped by) and then choose what I liked! I bought some groovy stuff, I can tell you. The other big thing was the carpet in the limo – I like having bare feet, so the fluffy floor was fabulous. There were no seatbelts, so I could stretch out and sleep on the journey home. Oh – and the show was some of the best acting I've seen – and Tim loved it, and he's picky. Altogether a brilliant birthday. My sister Dee babysat for Caitlin, who is very clingy at present, so it was good having someone from the family looking after her. My final birthday present was the arrival of my laptop fresh from Holland – it came this morning.

The only down point was after the shopping thing – which was a glimpse of how the super-rich live – we were eating an early pre-theatre dinner, and I suddenly got so sad. It was poignant that here I was, living a day that most women would say they would 'die for' and all day I'd been trying to shake off a dream wherein I died. The dream was very real and very painful, but in it all I wanted was to die in Tim's arms – the dream was about trying to get to him.

The show broke the mood and this morning I have been twirling in my new dresses, trying not to fall over, feeling happy and beautiful again. Today I know that I will dance towards death, but not for a while yet.

Her birthday was a massive thing for me. It had to be amazing – not just great or fine, but amazing. I needed her to know how much I loved her, how much I would do for her, how much I would spend on her. It all had to be bigger, more extravagant, more everything. I'm not really sure why. The day in London was stupidly over the top, it all cost too much and was too tiring for her. The day she really enjoyed was the day on the beach. It meant everything to her, to be somewhere she loved with the people she loved, feeling free. I watched her walk along the beach, the wind billowing her flowing chiffon dress, feeling the pleasure she felt of having the wet sand under her feet, squidging up around her toes. Then there was the water, the sea, the ocean stretching out to the horizon cleansing her, swallowing her cancer in its vastness. The sadness was a deep beautiful melancholy. We both felt it. At one point I walked past her, chasing after a friend's small child, and she grabbed my hand and gave it the briefest of all possible squeezes, and yet in that moment we said everything, it was all understood – this was the last birthday for her and for us.

The funniest thing that happened on the London day was bumping into George, Weeze's brother-in-law. He's a gorgeous big man, sweet as pie, with a heart of gold, salt of the earth, and loads of other hackneyed sayings, but he really is lovely. However, if you don't know him, his sheer height and scale can be intimidating and he does look a little like an East-end heavy. Well, both of us had tea in Harvey Nichols, then went along to the special rooms put aside for private shopping to see how Weeze was doing. As we entered the place, George put on his dark glasses and went into a full bodyguard routine. The problem was, he did it so well that the beautiful women swanning around Louise took him seriously and didn't bat an eyelid when he kept saying things like 'Sir, I think the building is secure', and then he'd talk into the imaginary microphone in his lapel and say 'Estimated ETA of subject twenty minutes. The pig is in the poke.' He refused to sit down and paced forwards and backwards observing everyone in a particularly intimidating way. Occasionally he'd peer suspiciously through the curtains out on to the street or scan the rooftops looking for snipers. As soon as we left we cracked up.

7 August

I guess it's only to be expected that I should feel a little down after such an exciting week. The clothes are still great, but the mood is definitely less ebullient than of late. I've been having some horrid dreams. I suppose that my subconscious needs some time to work out the fears, and I'm not giving it much space in my life. I have often wondered what forms our demons would take if we had never seen any television or films – Death was Jabba the Hut in one of last night's scenarios! It sounds comical now, but it wasn't then, I can tell you . . . His computer-generated self looked very wrong in my bedroom.

Today we drove down to Dungeness and looked at some very desolate wind-blown houses – including the late director Derek Jarman's and his fabulous garden of strange rock patterns and driftwood sculptures. I felt ill most of the day – sometimes sick, sometimes in pain, sometimes just ill. There are just days when I do feel like I am dying of cancer, just as there are days I can hardly believe I'm ill at all. At least I talked to Caitlin a lot today. We were in the back of the car together and we played lots of games and told stories where we take it in turns to do the next bit. I'm constantly amazed by her. She has a perfect grasp of the structure of stories. When she was tiny and I was breastfeeding I felt that we were still connected by an invisible umbilicus; I feel that way again now. We are both overly emotional and clingy – all three of us, in fact. We all want to be together all the time and yet we long for some space to be ourselves and to create. Tim and I give each other space to work and then find ourselves missing each other too much to be productive; Caitlin longs to play with friends but wants us both to come too. We are all feeling our way through an emotional maze, but I have the proverbial 'blind faith' that we will cope with whatever we must deal with.

9 August

Felt utterly, utterly crap today. Lots of pain and a real difficulty in opening my eyes, let alone getting up. In the end I surfaced at 6.30 p.m., coming down in time to watch *The Simpsons* with Caitlin. My hospice nurse, Catherine, came round and we had a good chat . . . my first proper talk about dying with someone who has witnessed the grand event. She put some of my fears at rest re. dying alone, not being able to breathe and dying in pain or anxiety. I am certainly not against drugs – they saw me through childbirth, they'll see me through death. My mother and Tim's dad, both of whom came round today, have promised to sit and hold my hand all night when the end nears, and the hospice have nurses on call twenty-four hours a day. To be held and told that everything is OK ... isn't that what everyone wants at numerous difficult points in their lives?

Anyway, I'm glad the topic has been broached ... she asked if I would rather die at home or in the hospice, and I said at home, depending on my condition and if it got too upsetting for Caitlin and/or Tim. Maybe now I've addressed the issue during the hours of daylight, it will leave me alone at night ...

These are difficult conversations, and I'm guessing it doesn't take a brain surgeon to work that out. To actually discuss in the cold light of day the way in which you want to die, who you want to be there and where you want to be, is something that nobody ever tells you would occur. I really enjoyed my schooldays, and my time at university, but unless I missed the class I don't ever remember any of my teachers or lecturers saying to me, 'OK, when it comes to the time when your wife is dying and she's lying on her death bed discussing the ways she wants to die, these are the main things it's important to say in order to be a sensitive and caring man ...' Whenever Weeze brought up the subject of the last few minutes of her life, I wanted to start singing or shouting or anything to drown out the sound of her voice. I knew it was going to happen and it was becoming increasingly obvious that it was going to happen sooner rather than later, but I didn't want to have to visualize the last moment. I felt scared of it and couldn't believe how calm everyone else seemed when this subject came up. Maybe they were all as freaked out as me, but they did a great job of hiding it.

What it came down to was the simple fact that Weeze had always said and made me promise that when she died I'd be there holding her hand and the truth that I never told Weeze was that I couldn't do it, I just couldn't sit there and watch her go. Whenever I said I'd do it, all I could think was, 'No, it's not going to happen, I'm not going to be there, I'll do anything to not be there.' It was utter fear. I saw it as the big test, not of our love, but of myself, of me. Would I be able to overcome this dreadful horror and do the only thing my wife had ever made me swear I'd do?

10 August

I have had two emails recently which could both be answered with the same train of thought. One was from someone who isn't ill and it asked me what I'm like aside from the cancer i.e. what are my favourite TV programmes, films, etc. The other was from the girl who sparked off another entry recently; hers asked me if everything in my whole life reflects the fact that I have cancer.

Yes, is the answer. When I first started writing this diary people who knew me well said, 'Yes, it's you, but only the "you-with-cancer" you.' Now I think I am the 'me-with-cancer' me. Everything I do is done from the point of view of someone who is ill, with a limited time frame. This doesn't mean I'm miserable all the time, it just means I try to make everything I do count. Even if it's lying on the floor playing with Caitlin, it's important. I have very little time for television now, so no, I don't really have a favourite show any more. When I'm tired and lying on Tim's shoulders I like to watch stuff that makes me laugh – *The Larry Sanders Show* springs to mind, for one. Otherwise I like films, but if they're unsatisfying or longer than 1 hour 45 mins I get cross with them for wasting my time. Music can still transport me – and by that I really mean remove me from pain, physical and emotional. It can also make me weep. Gram Parsons and James Taylor are my two favourites, I guess.

I don't get up before midday now – if I do I'm sick and then I have to take another pill and go back to bed until it works. I have morphine-releasing patches on my back (so I can wear my lovely new clothes without horrible plastic things on my arms). I like to have people around in the house somewhere, even though I like to be alone. I like to spend an hour or two doing this a day. My life is so unlike a twenty-eight-year-old mother's life would normally be, that I cannot really forget, ever. I'm reading a funny book at the moment called *Sex and Sunsets* by Tim Sandling – I find laughter, as always, the best thing for almost any situation, and the hero seems to have worse luck than I do! My mother read me a good chunk of the book today, whilst I lay in bed. Mothers are the best for that, aren't they?

Why is it that when major events happen everything in the whole universe seems to relate to it? For example, when I was fifteen, I had one terrifying week thinking I'd got my then girlfriend pregnant. Every telly programme, advert, book I read, was about being pregnant. It was like some cosmic joke, and this fabulous sense of fantastical humour continued into our cancer life. Before Weeze was diagnosed with cancer I don't think I ever saw a film or read a book about anyone who had cancer, then suddenly I couldn't get away from it. I'd read the back of a video, and it would say something like, 'Quirky comedy about a man and a woman in love.' And what it would turn out to be was 'A depressing story about a bunch of people whose lives are destroyed by a brain tumour, which leaves either the husband or the wife alone looking after a small blonde child with blue eyes who makes your heart melt and they'll never really recover, they'll just crumble into a ghost life of non-existence.' It was the same with books. I used to regularly buy Weeze novels, to cheer her up. But I managed to buy three books in a row which all had someone dying of cancer – one even had the main young heroine dying of a brain tumour in her early thirties. Now, either when I picked these books up I just didn't notice the massive sign saying: WARNING THIS BOOK WILL SEEM TOO POIGNANT FOR YOU IF YOU'VE GOT CANCER, or – as I suspect – cancer isn't a great selling point on the back cover. Ooops, doesn't bode well for this book, then.

13 August

I've been ill for a couple of days. Lots of pain and lots of sleeping, so I haven't felt like writing. Today I dragged myself out of bed to see my nephew, Harry, and his friend who are on their way down to Brighton. Brighton is the happening place at the moment – if nineteen-year-olds think it's cool, as well as us old fogies, it must be. It was strange seeing them. I wished Tim was around, as he's better at talking about music and stuff to younger people. I was also desperate not to appear scary to them — an aunt with an eye-patch and a terminal illness may not impress the friend. But they were both sweet and easy to talk to. I think nervous at first, then more relaxed. Which is how I think most people respond to me; not knowing what to say or how to be until we all relax a bit. It is as though the cancer has made me a different person — which it has — and so people are shy at first and have to get to know this new person all over again. When I wasn't so obviously ill people said, 'I was nervous at first to see you, knowing you're ill, but then I realized you're still the same old Louise.' Now that I don't feel I am the same old Louise, there is a new kind of nervousness between myself and many people. Particularly people I have not seen for a long time. I am nervous about how they will react to me, they are nervous about how I will be. I don't know if they mind me talking about being ill, they don't know if I want to talk about it or not.

The doorbell rang and I've just come back to the computer and re-read the above. Boring, boring. Blah, blah. I'm bored of cancer now. I've had enough, thank you, Mr God, and would like it to go away. The doorbell was my hospice nurse and we had a lovely chat. I told her how Tim and I fell in love and it made me feel so soppy and romantic and in love. And lucky. Talking about cancer now seems wrong — like being given a flower and going on and on about the one brown petal instead of the loads of golden ones. However, talking to the nurse has made my tongue hurt, so I shall load this up and go to bed for a bit. Ciao.

14 August

Someone came round today and asked if they could buy a photograph to put on the wall of their new house. I was over the moon. They really want to put something I did on the wall? It got me re-fired up about doing an exhibition. My eternal List of Things To Do gets continually re-prioritized. My current Top 10 includes:

Exhibition (perhaps 'ex-(in)hibition'?)

Caitlin Book (new format – best So Far . . .)

Cookery Video (yes, I know, I still haven't though . . .)

Doing little love-notes for Tim and leaving them scattered about the house in books and things for him to keep finding for years . . . fortunately he very rarely reads this, so it should remain a secret, so long as you don't tell . . .

You may detect a certain frivolous tone to my writing this evening. If so, well done Sherlock, for I am in an ebullient mood. A tricky word to attempt without a spell-check or the knowledge to put the damn thing back on . . . the reason for this light-heartedness is a narrow escape from an untimely death. Last night I received a mis-labelled bottle of morphine from my chemist. I realized that it was mis-labelled and tried to work out the dose for myself. I then had a minor panic-attack, having convinced myself that I had overdosed. So, down to the local Accident & Emergency, tight-chested and short of breath. Caitlin and Tim in the car, Tim's father on the way. I felt exactly as I do when I'm dying in my dreams. By the time I'd run through the story with a nurse, then a doctor, I was fine, if a little weepy and shaky. Tim and I were both convinced I was going to spend the weekend in intensive care.

Instead we have been entertaining our normal stream of visitors and hugging each other extra tightly. We're not quite ready yet. Still, I'm glad I get these little reminders every now and again, because it keeps me focused on The List.

To say that this made me angry would have been an under-statement. There are times when everything is bad enough without a chemist giving you the wrong prescription. I'm not sure whether I'm legally allowed to say who it was, but let's just say 'Not shoes . . .' The worst thing about it is that half my life was spent running around getting differ-ent drugs from all over town. Most mornings I'd be handed a new prescription by one doctor or another and off I'd trog up to town and – ludicrous as it might sound – it could often take me up to three hours to get everything on the list. Being a natural hypochondriac, sitting with a load of coughing and wheezing souls who also have to wait half an hour for their drugs to come through is my idea of torture.

The other thing that particularly pissed me off about the whole thing was that every time I went in to get Weeze's medicine they made me feel like a criminal. 'You know this is a controlled substance, Sir?' They'd always say this in a kind of whisper, maybe because they were being sensi-tive and didn't think I'd want anybody to know that my wife was a terminally ill junky, but it just made it feel illicit, as if I was doing something wrong. And the times that there was a slight mistake on the prescription and they'd make me walk all the way to the surgery to get it rectified were innumerable. But I put up with all of this in reason-able good humour because I presumed they were only doing their jobs and that these petty regulations were in place so that screw-ups didn't happen. However, when they totally mis-label a potentially lethal drug and hand it out, it's enough to make you scream. Luckily both Weeze and I were very clued up on dosages so nothing disastrous actually happened. It wasn't made better by the reaction of the shop in question when I calmly and pleasantly phoned them up first thing Monday morning to inform them that they'd screwed up and nearly killed my wife. 'Thank you, sir, we'll look into it.' That was it, no 'Terribly sorry, how can we possibly grovel enough? What can we do to make the awful heartache you and your good lady wife have been through better?' Nothing. And did we hear from them again? No-siree-Bob. I know they're human and everybody makes mistakes, but the least they could have done was apologize and take responsibility for their actions.

These are really small things but they matter, because life's short and when you're living with a ticking time bomb waiting for it to blow-up and ruin your life, what you don't need is to deal with ungracious people. OK, grizzle over.

17 August

Everything is a huge effort. I'm ill – possibly flu or something. I'm having dreadful nightmares and my usual way of approaching death seems to have abandoned me. Yesterday was the first time I've moaned out loud that I'm dying and that I can't cope with it all. Sorry if that's too heavy, guys, you are under no obligation to follow me all the way on this journey.

Today I feel a tiny bit better – at least I can see that feelings like this won't last. After all, nothing does ... I want to be a little girl again, in a world of grown-ups who know what to do all the time and have the power to make everything all right. I miss the seventies and want to surround myself with brown hessian and shag-pile carpets. That's half a joke and half real. Tim's downstairs working out the music for a drama production of *Oh What a Lovely War* and he's playing music from around the First World War. It's the kind of music my father played around the house as I was growing up and it's making me feel all nostalgic.

Still getting nightmares, so the hospice counsellor, Vincent, is coming to see me this afternoon. He's very nice. I'm on a truckload of drugs now: antibiotics, pain killers, tablets for nausea, valium for anxiety caused by nightmares ... I think that's it. I feel a little better now, compared to when I started writing this. I still feel that this means there is a purpose to all this. Otherwise it is a little bleak. Thank you all for being out there and for listening.

After Weeze died all I wanted was someone who could make everything better. I wanted to find a giant mum. A mother in scale to me now, who could wrap me up in her arms, hold me tight and smother me with love. I wanted the smell of a mum to soothe me like it had when I was a baby. Some things are just too big to face alone, you just don't feel grown-up enough to have to burden the weight of them. My own mum was great and supportive and strong and everything she could have been, but it wasn't my mum that I needed, it was some universal mother figure, something bigger, God perhaps.

18 August

Well, Vincent, the counsellor, was lovely and helped me talk through a few of my nightmares and fears. Caitlin's out all day today, so Tim has a bit of space, even if I spend all day in bed again. One of the things we talked about with Vincent was the need for him to have outlets: at the moment he's trying to run a house, be a full-time father, keep something of his career going AND look after a dying wife. Stressful stuff.

I'm now out of bed at least, but still feeling pretty crap. We seem to have jigged our finances around to enable the flat in Brighton idea to become a reality. At times it's hard for me to imagine being well enough to even look around houses, let alone decorate one, but then I think it's really important that I have something to look forward to that isn't too hard.

I want to mention here how *extremely* grateful I am for all the emails and guest book entries I get. Today I really had to drag myself out of bed to load this up and I looked at my mail and the site for the first time in a few days. It restored my faith in myself. Thank you.

19 August

Feeling a little brighter today – certainly emotionally, if not a great deal physically better. Bottom line is, this is how ill I am and I can either wallow in it and have no more nice memories from now on, or I can try to enjoy the times I feel a little better. So 'Smile, though your heart is breaking', as the song says. No, that's overly melodramatic, my heart isn't breaking – I'm still surrounded by more love than almost anyone I know.

Tim took Caitlin to Brighton this morning to get details from estate agents – it's all a bit more expensive than we'd thought, but it gives us something to plan and I like looking through papers and circling things, day-dreaming. I've been upright for five hours now and still feeling good – that's better than the rest of this week. Whenever I start filling the dishwasher and tutting about the state of the kitchen floor, I know I'm on the mend – when you're really ill, you just don't care. I'm also back to caring how I look a bit and wanting to do stuff again – wanting to do lots of stuff with Caitlin. I've spent a little bit of time playing with some of my pictures on Photoshop, but I'm afraid I still don't know how to put them on the site. My 'webmaster' Gavin came down to teach me on Monday, but I was too ill to get out of bed. Patience, patience.

Later

I feel fantastic. Partly just because the weather's lightened and I feel good and partly because it is such a huge relief. That the antibiotics have worked, that *This isn't It*. Caitlin sat on my lap all through dinner tonight, two days after I'd been talking to a counsellor about relinquishing my role as a mother because maybe now I was too ill. I'm like an over-excited child with too much energy – it's 11.30 and I ought to go to sleep so that I'm well enough to look at flats tomorrow in Brighton, but instead I want to plan my photography exhibition (well, the first couple at least), I want to imagine my interviews on the radio as I plug my book (this site as a book, perhaps?), I want to unfurl my wings again. When I was ill and trying to shake off the nightmares I started doing a visualization where I was a glorious golden bird inside this broken-down body and that death, rather than being scary, would be a release into flight. Now I feel that the real inner me has perked up and shaken off the artificial golden eagle. The eagle was too perfect and golden. Somewhere inside me is a bird of rather more straggly feathers, but far more interesting character.

The golden bird would feature again very prominently in my life over the following months. I had never heard of

it before one night in November, and now I see that the whole world knew of its existence before me. Maybe I should have read this diary after all before now. I'm finding it constantly surprising how much there was going on in Weeze's head that I was unaware of. I think, because we were so close, I assumed I knew everything that she was thinking. But, of course, I didn't, as she didn't know everything that was going on in mine. There's a song by Kate Bush which, as I understand, says that you could only really know the person you love if God could allow you to swap places with them and actually be them for a time to know how they were feeling. With Weeze, I knew her on a spiritual level. OK, I might not have known some of the smaller details, or even the bigger theories running through her head, but I knew her soul inside and out, and she knew mine, and so she should have done – she stole it and kept it locked up in her heart from the moment we first kissed.

21 August

Yesterday was a really amazing day in lots of ways. I am paying for it today, mind you, but here's a glimpse of why it was worth it. Firstly, I got up at 8.30 a.m. for the first time in about a month, then we went down to Brighton and viewed five flats and then . . . bought one! Well, nothing's paid for, but our offer was accepted. Like true love, I just knew and so we went for it. It's right on the coast and is sweet. It needs no work and has two titchy bedrooms – just right for weekends on the beach.

Then we finally went on our balloon flight! We'd had it cancelled so many times that I stopped telling people about it and then it happened. It felt like a confirmation from on high that the flat was right. I LOVED the flight. Everything looked so peaceful. It made me realize how toy-like and insignificant man and his structures are. The houses, cars, towns all looked so small. The sunset was amazing. There was a time when I had to resist the urge to jump out – it looked like a far more fun way to die than some others I can think of, but that wore off.

That golden eagle thing I was talking about in my last entry. Call me flaky, but I've been thinking more about it. It is very calming for me to think of a spiritual part of me inside myself that will come into its own when I die. To be able to visualize this part helps it feel real. When I was having some counselling years ago I worked on seeing and talking to different aspects of myself and it was interesting. My ideal life after death thing would be if my consciousness left my broken-down body and entered the bird part of me (I see it like a puppet phoenix – maybe an image from childhood). The phoenix (literally rising from the ashes) would have all the answers to *everything* and the wider knowledge I would possess would mean I would no longer be attached to Earth – or at least suffer loss or separation from people here now. Meditating along these lines has, I think, helped me stop the nightmares. Big thanks to Tim – he used to have nightmares and has helped me.

Now this entry amazes me! Talk about understatement, Weezy! The day before wasn't just an amazing day, it was mind-blowing, it was one of the days of my married life. As with a lot of things we did in the last year, in order to support Weeze in the things she wanted to do I had to face my fears and conquer them. The balloon flight was one such thing. As you know by now, I'm not a great one for flying at the best of times, and that's when it's in a big metal plane, let alone when it's in a flimsy basket held up only by an even flimsier piece of silk.

The day started out like any other. We went down to Brighton and looked round for some flats. Most we saw were awful, nasty, poky little things that smelt damp and dark. Then finally Weeze heard of a flat that wasn't even officially on the market yet and was told we could only go and see it from the outside. So we drove round to the street and the house it's in looked so sweet and dinky that Weeze fell in love with it straight away. As luck would have it, the owner was having some new carpets put in and Weeze jumped out of the car and followed one of the carpet men up the stairs and managed to charm her way into the flat for a look around. Two minutes later she was out in the car again reaching for the mobile.

'Hi there, it's Mrs Arthur. The property in Queensbury Mews, yeah that's the one, I know it hasn't come on the market strictly speaking, but I'll take it. Yes, that's what I said, I'll take it. At the full asking price, and I shall be paying in cash.'

She then gave a large sigh of satisfaction and rested her head back on the headrest. After a minute I think she remembered she wasn't alone and opened her eyes to look at the incredulous husband beside her. 'You'll like it, honestly. It's lovely.'

I made some mumbling sound about how I wouldn't have minded having a say, and she just smiled and stroked my cheek. The deal was done and she was right, I trusted her. I saw the flat a couple of day later and it was very cute.

So we left Brighton one flat the richer, several thousand pounds the poorer, and headed for home. On the way

Weeze phoned up the balloon people to check on the weather conditions. I prayed that the wind would be up and that all flying would be off, but no such luck. As she clicked the phone off and turned to me and said, 'It's on, Tim, we're actually going to do it tonight,' my heart sank and butterflies the size of elephants started jumping around in my stomach.

It was a beautiful evening for flying and as we arrived at the field I was hoping desperately that the tactics of turning up half an hour late would mean that we'd missed it but, again, no such luck. The magnificent balloon was lying on its side and was waiting in eager anticipation to be filled with hot air. At that moment I decided I wasn't going, it was all too much. I didn't need that kind of stress. My dad was there and he'd offered to stand in for me at the last minute if I felt I couldn't do it. I couldn't do it, I knew I couldn't do it, so I wasn't going to do it.

It took about half an hour to get the balloon inflated and I helped hold the opening open so that the giant fan could blow the thing up. It was so beautiful. Looking at the inside of the balloon as it rippled its way into life was exquisite, it looked like a whole other world where the sea was bright red and tempest-tossed and the sky was a gentle undulating, pulsating light sunset orange. I think it was at that point that I knew I'd go, but I didn't admit it to myself in order to hold off the nerves. Weeze came over and hugged me and watched the ever-expanding landscape over my shoulder. She kissed my neck and sealed the deal. When it was fully inflated and everyone else was in, I helped Weeze to climb aboard. Then, without even looking round for a substitute, I climbed in and we were off.

Slowly, slowly, silently, silently, the world below moved

away from us as we waved it goodbye. Both our dads and Caitlin became tiny silhouette models of people mechanically gesturing in a painted field. The fear I had been expecting was dispelled by beauty. The most poetic of sunsets had been emblazoned on the sky, gold and pink tones washed over the world and made everything magical. Although there were another eight people in the tiny basket with us, we were alone and holding each other. There was a release about the soft movement of the balloon. The fact that the balloon is led to its destination by the wind means you're in Nature's hands, vulnerable and trusting in the Mother, believing she'll keep you safe, show you her magnificence. And she did. As we climbed to five thousand feet, the air became colder and we snuggled in tighter, looking out at our world, wondering at it. Neither of us spoke for the whole hour we were in the air, we simply opened our souls and let our love experience the ride. It was at times exhilarating, at times melancholic. As I kissed the back of Weeze's neck I could feel her sadness – she was looking out on a world she was leaving. The hour went by like a dream, but like all dreams you have to wake up and we came back to the ground with a bump, in more ways than one.

23 August

Tomorrow I have a meeting with Prof Gleeson. It's been a long time and I'm nervous. I doubt whether he'll be able to tell me the answer to my main, glaringly obvious question, but of anyone on this earth, he can.

I've been taking a lot of pictures recently on my digital camera. When I allow myself to daydream about what might have been, it is often about photography. I don't want to sound big-headed, but I can feel that there is an artist inside me. One of my few regrets is that I didn't discover it earlier. I'm beginning to have the confidence that artists have (or I assume them to have) – the confidence to decide what makes a good picture regardless of whether it is in focus or not, etc.

On the other hand, maybe that's one of the many things I would never have grasped had I not become ill. Confidence in my judgement, confidence in who I am. Some people seem to be born with it – true belief in who they are. I think that most confident people aren't really sure who they are and live in secret fear that they will somehow be 'found out'. This is one of the greatest stresses a person can live under. I think that loads of people, millions, live their whole lives like that. One of the annoying things about clichés is that they are so bloody true. It sounds so trite to say 'be yourself'. But the relief that you feel and the confidence to be gained by really living honestly, by being yourself and not giving a damn, is amazing. I heartily recommend it. In the past I would have taken something like photography and not have had the balls to really go for it – because I haven't got an art degree I wouldn't have trusted myself to become an artist. I'm rambling as usual, but the point is, I am more happy with myself as a person than I ever have been before – the secret is to get there without having to have cancer. At least I've got there in my lifetime. I'll write tomorrow and tell you what the latest prognosis is, if there is any news. In the meantime, believe in yourselves . . .

24 August

I haven't been up to London yet – just got up earlier than usual. Tim and Caitlin are in Brighton (checking that the flat still looks like a good idea in the rain!) and I felt like writing. A friend of mine recently went through a tough time and I was so wrapped up in myself that a week went by before I really asked her how she was. I think I have become a little self-centred (my mother's fears came true) and, partly because of the website, I tend to assume that everybody wants to know how *I* am all the time. Sometimes the cyber-world – me soliloquizing and you lot listening – becomes confused with the real world – people I know who have problems of their own, who need me to listen to them. Anyway, I have resolved to be a better listener and stop thinking so much about myself.

Tim has bought a skateboard. I'm so proud of him. Loads of men of his age that we know would love one, but he just went and bought one. He skates around our park, nodding to all the groups of fourteen-year-olds. It's really funny. The guys in the shop asked when he last skated. '1978,' he said. 'Wow, you were part of the first wave, dude.' Well, they probably didn't actually say dude, but in my head people who work in skate shops all say dude. Caitlin loves the board and sits on it, scooting herself around the park with her feet, piling sticks and leaves in front of her. 'This board is good for my collections,' she says, 'these are just my bits and bobs.'

Later

Just got back from Guy's. The meeting with Prof Gleeson was great – we talked cameras as usual, but he was also very positive about my health. I feel great and he seems to think I've got time to do a lot more writing and taking pictures yet. Also some other news – I've heard today from a national newspaper about doing something on this site / me and Tim. We shall see what transpires. Anyway, after the positive meeting I'm too buzzed to sit and type, so I'm off.

25 August

A physical breakthrough! Today I did some old yoga and T'ai Chi stretches that I used to do and I realized that I've been totally out of touch with my body. Perhaps (if it doesn't sound too flaky) I've been angry with my body. (I wonder why on earth that would be?) Anyway, for the last year or so, I have been tired and overweight and generally lacking in oomph and physical self-esteem. Finally (for all the wrong reasons, of course) I have lost weight and feel great about myself, so I'm feeling a lot more friendly towards my physical self. I've decided to start doing more gentle exercise – nothing sweaty or too tiring but something stretchy to make me feel fitter. Along with a decline in anger towards my body comes a decline in anger towards my cancer. I reckon we can co-exist happily for another year or so to allow me to get a load more done before I go. After all, the cancer cells are only bits of me that are growing too fast in the wrong direction, as I tell Caitlin. More to be pitied than hated, really.

That's the weird thing about cancer, it's your own cells killing you. It's not some foreign body attacking you, it's you doing it. I think that's why so many New Agers put it down to self-loathing and childhood guilt and one hundred and one other such things. The analogy is just too perfect – if your body is killing itself there must be a reason for it, it must be physically responding to emotions which you're not facing but are internalizing. Here's my problem with this theory – it seems like an extreme way for the body to gain attention. As soon as we are born or created, the goal of all living organisms is to live for as long as they can to further their species through procreation, protection and growth. These things are the most powerful forces in the world. So why then would the body override these urges and say, 'Well, rather than let this uptight person go on I think we should kill it off.' I know I've got the wrong end of the stick and a thousand and one people who believe in the energetic bodies will be calling me obtuse, but I'm doing it on purpose, just to wind you guys up – oh, go on, give us a smile. Don't take everything so seriously.

27 August

We did the newspaper interview. It threw up some strange feelings and some large questions, along the lines of Why am I really doing this website? And do I really want to be 'famous' with all that that entails, with its repercussions for Tim and Caitlin? It's all very well for me, living my life at home, in bed half the time, knowing that more people will read the diary. But what about Tim, who goes out into the real world, teaching drama to kids whose parents all read papers? What about Caitlin who goes to school with kids whose parents all read papers? I'm regretting it already and it hasn't even come out yet.

I don't know what I'm doing. I'm afraid that this diary is all an act, a persona. It's the side of me that is coping well – but only because I'm writing does it seem like that. The act of writing immediately distances me from my emotions. It is far easier to write than to really feel. What I leave unsaid are all the bits between. This huge ball of pain that sits in the middle of our family, being skirted around like a pit in the middle of the sitting room. No one wants to 'be' with it, to cry properly and really feel it. Does that mean we're 'coping well' as we are continually told, or does it mean we're in denial and are coping far, far less well than a family who sits around crying all day? I don't know and I doubt anyone has the answers really. I certainly don't feel I have the answers to anything at the moment.

You cope with things as well as you can and that's it. With something of this magnitude, who cares even if you are faking it. If it means you can get through another day then I think you're just finding a way of being. After all, it's not as if Weeze had to worry about future repercussions. When she was down, she was down, and when she was up, she was up, and when she was only halfway up, she was neither up nor down. What Weeze did achieve through her strength, even if it was some kind of denial, was make life liveable for all those around her. In the last two months of her life she hit a hideous depression and it made it harder for everyone – for me, for Caitlin, for our parents, our friends whom she no longer wanted to see, everyone. If denial gets you through a long period without having to hit the darkness, then all well and good, let's all live in denial for as long as we can before the crushing knowledge of our own mortality really grasps us and we are faced with the truth – we are all born to die.

29 August

If, by some remote chance, it escaped anyone's attention, I was rather down yesterday. Physically and emotionally. Yesterday, however, I had a very constructive chat with my hospice nurse, a doctor and Tim. I realized a couple of things. Firstly,

I think that I was translating the media stuff (and this, too, a little) into pressure to be seen to be coping brilliantly all the time. I have now come to grips with the fact that any value this diary may have is not to do with how well I cope or not, but to do with my ability to express in words that others can identify with how I'm feeling. I think the media stuff is fine now, as the pressure feels off me. I'm only doing it so that more people can hear about the site and I do think the diary is a good thing. There, that's got all that off my chest.

The second thing I realized was quite how interlinked my body is with my emotions. When I get depressed, I throw up. I feel as though I need to physically reject the feelings. I also stop being able to eat. As soon as I expressed these feelings, I felt loads better and, really feeling the support that was around me, I was able to eat and then to get up and go to the park to watch Tim and Caitlin skateboarding. It was so clear. Emotional comfort = physical comfort. I was talking to my mother last night and she said that I have always reacted physically to emotions. I especially remember a boyfriend who dumped me when I was about sixteen. It wasn't love or anything, but my pride was very hurt, and I sweated and threw up all night – I remember feeling I wanted to get the feeling of rejection out of me. My mum sat with me in the spare bedroom all night, telling me stories and stroking my head. I had forgotten it until now. I was fine in the morning. It did occur to me that perhaps the New Age types are right and if being dumped by a boyfriend can make you throw up then perhaps something can make you self-destruct on a cancer level, but as I have no idea what that something could have been or how to sort it out, I don't really know how it helps at the moment. Maybe it will come to me out of the blue. (And I thought I'd finished with all that hope malarky!) Aah, well, it is a long journey with many different states of mind along the way.

Later

Either my state of mind has had a dramatic effect on my health, or the combination of drugs I'm on is really working. This morning I got up early and had a really good bath. A well-paced day also – lunch with a lovely family where I played farms happily with the children, then home for some quiet 'cut and stick' time with Caitlin, then a rest before Tim goes out to the cinema with some friends. I decided I would stay in and have an early night (as well as doing make-up with Caitlin) and I asked for an hour's rest first. These are all good signs – me knowing my limitations, enjoying 'normal' life and motherhood. I feel I know who I am again and am comfortable with it.

OK, so she got nervous and threw up, and then did a flip about face and thought maybe the emotions did effect the way you were physically, and that maybe that had actually caused her cancer. And now I feel a little silly – see, maybe I should read forward before I write. But at least you know you're reading what I'm writing. I still think she's wrong though, even though I'm currently very stressed and my arms have suddenly developed the most terrible eczema. For all that, I'm still telling you my wife didn't kill herself, and her spirit was pure and her body just fucked up – it was no one's fault, it was just shitty stuff.

30 August

I feel as though I'm finding a level again. Tim is working hard on *Oh What a Lovely War* for the next couple of weeks and Caitlin goes back to school a week tomorrow, so some sense of routine is returning to the family. And with it a certain security. Children are supposed to feel safer and more secure with routine and I think the same goes for adults during times of stress. When you are feeling strong and well it is all very well to live a random, carefree life, but when you are low I think routine gives support. Which is why institutions like monasteries, hospitals and schools are so addictive – they provide a framework to your life which relieves you of a whole plethora of decisions. When I went to stay in a Buddhist monastery for a retreat I found it s-o-o-o relaxing. Not to have to even think about when to eat, sleep, get up, what to do with all but an hour or so's free time a day. It released my mind from so many mundane thoughts. As a mother you have to generally set the timetable for everyone in the family, which is a constant responsibility. Tim and I have been passing it back and forth between us, but it is easier when it is done for you by outside influences like work and school. I'm sure that's one of the reasons I enjoyed my stay in the hospice.

This afternoon a photographer is coming to take our picture for the newspaper article. The paper is the *Independent* and it comes out next Monday. I've forgotten everything I said to them. I hope it comes out OK. At least they are definitely putting the site address in so people can read the whole picture. I'm feeling so much more grounded and comfortable with myself the last few days. I shall be off now and choose something to wear, maybe the dress that's on this home page – it's still my favourite at the moment. Bye.

The *Independent* photographer was great. He took really fun pictures – some of just Tim and me, some of the three of us. In some we were sitting on the kitchen table and in some we were bouncing on our bed. I defy anyone to write a miserable article on the strength of those pictures. He also said he'd send us the negatives, which is really nice, so we'll have some good pictures of the two / three of us. It was fun. I laughed lots. Tim wore a shirt he bought in New York that I think makes him look like a gay clubber – it's made of blue sequins. He wore it because I said I never wanted to be seen in public with him in it – so he chooses a national paper to wear it for the first time! Don'tcha just love him? I do.

This evening we watched a documentary on an English writer / character called Jeffery Bernard. I loved it. He is witty, drunk, miserably bleak, honest ... I like him, but I also feel great that I'm me, not him. He is old age. Old age as I don't ever want to see it. There is something to be said for not living past all the relationships in your life, for quitting while you're ahead. I remember how desperately unhappy so many of the people I've been in hospital with looked. I don't want to ever look at my hands and see them replaced by old hands I don't recognize.

Later

I've just had a very constructive day doing all the boring paperwork I've been putting off for weeks. It always makes me feel organized and more relaxed when I've cleared up the little things that niggle away at the back of my mind, needing to be done. I then found out how to get my 'web statistics' – in other words, how many people check this site out. So far it's had over 50,000 hits!!!! I'm *extremely* excited. You can see it all as graphs and see how many people check in on any given day. 3 p.m. seems to be a popular time. Weekdays too are busier – I guess because lots of people log on from work.

I had a chat to Catherine, my hospice nurse, about the steroids I'm on – I wanted to make sure my cheerful mood was not completely drug-induced. We worked out that I've probably got a kick from them, but that my depression of last week lifted before I started taking them – after I talked things through with Tim, really. It feels more comfortable to think that I'm still in charge of my emotions, rather than being at the mercy of tablets. My current mix finds me pain-free without being sleepy, which is perfect.

As Weeze got more and more ill, the amount of drugs she was taking went up almost daily, or so it seemed, and the thing about drugs is they do stuff to you. Sometimes they make you feel good, sometimes they make you feel crap, sometimes they stop you feeling anything at all. Weeze's drugs made her feel loads of things and the cancer made her feel loads of things, and I made her feel loads of things, and Caitlin made her feel loads of things – all in all, the poor girl had a lot of things going on with her. It meant that her moods were unpredictable at the best of times. She was nearly always loving but often found it difficult to just rest or relax, unless she was so ill that she had no choice about it. But she could get angry, upset, morbid, hyper, all in the space of an hour. She was never sure what was her and what was everything else, and neither was I. It was very difficult to know how to handle her through everything. Sometimes you just had to hug her and kiss her, sometimes you had to listen to her while she ranted, other times you had to tell her what to do to give her boundaries and rules, other times you had to tell her off to shake her out of a particular mood. But the problem was you could do the wrong thing, push her when she needed hugging, hug her when she needed pushing, and you were in a worse position than you had been at the start.

Chapter 9

—

2 September

At the beginning of July I wrote about the start of a new month being once exciting, now depressing as time flashes by me. This time, starting a new page, I feel proud to be doing so well. Over the last couple of months I have retrieved bits of my life – my sweet taste buds are returning and now I wear the eye patch I no longer fall over. Just two months ago I was falling over about ten times a day. Re-reading that, it strikes me that it's wrong – I haven't retrieved anything. My taste buds have come back, yes, and the hospice staff gave me an eye patch – all very nice, but not much to do with me.

People always talk about fighting in connection with cancer, don't they? – 'She lost her long battle with cancer' – but I don't feel that way about it. How do you fight it? You fight to keep yourself as whole as possible throughout the experi-

—

201

ence, but I don't feel aggressive towards the cancer. Next time someone asks me how I'm fighting the cancer I shall raise my one visible eyebrow enigmatically and say 'On the beaches', before sweeping off as if to do battle.

Talking of which, a doctor lent me a book called *A Singular View* about living with one eye and the last page talks about Nelson and how he turned his disability into a heroic victory for England. The book ends with the words, 'Go, thou and do likewise.' Fabulous. I have been advised to carry a stick to help with the one-eyed thing and my father has one with a sword in it. Maybe I should carry that about and wave it around madly when talking about the cancer. A patch and a sword and the good excuse of the cancer being so close to my brain could liven up some parties.

The 'fighting' thing was a big issue for Weeze. It's really about attitude, I guess. She never felt that it was a fight because she didn't know what that actually meant. How can you fight to stay alive? She was much more into acceptance and this gave her a kind of peace. She accepted her illness and accepted she was going to die and, indeed, right towards the end she positively wanted to die – she had no clinging fear, she knew the game was up and wanted to retire gracefully from the field before the final painful checkmate. She was very much a person whose philosophy was, 'Well, you either live or you die, there's not much you can do about it.' She never really understood the big deal about it all. As she would constantly say, 'All of us are going to die sometime or another, what's the difference if it's now or when I'm eighty.' She knew she had lived a life, she'd experienced love, had a child, been creative and extraordinary and realized that many,

many people go through an entire life well into old age and never live, never experience half the things she did.

During our time with cancer we only met one other person with it, Weeze's sister, Dee, and she was very much on the same wavelength as us. We never met any other couples of our age who were going through it so we never really got to discuss how others feel, if others really approached it as a fight or if it was just one of those things that people say because they can't bear to think that someone could be dying and just accept it. The living love life – Weeze loved people but was quite ready to leave herself, her body.

3 September

Today three people have asked what I've been up to in a 'come on then, out with it' kind of way. With a smile. The first was a taxi driver and I answered with talk of shopping and the weather. The second two were shop assistants – I thought for a minute that I knew them. Then the penny dropped. Or rather the second shop assistant dropped it for me. 'I mean your eye. What have you gone and done?' Aaaah. The eye patch. Would you like the dying-of-cancer routine or would you rather an amusing tale involving mistaken identity and fishing rods? I'm sure Tim could rustle me up an anecdote to match every social occasion. Today I just didn't think of a witty answer and mumbled something about long-term problem and getting used to it. Something that embarrassed us both and ensured I left the shop quickly.

Caitlin is staying with Tim's mother, Toni, for two nights and so I browsed in bookshops all afternoon – something I don't usually have time for and greatly miss. In a minute

I'm going to have my hair bleached ... I never learn about hairdressers, do I? I shall let you know how it goes. Then tonight out to the cinema – Tim's working all weekend, so no romantic flips over to Paris, but I shall read lots and think lots and Caitlin will have a ball and be spoilt rotten. Must go now and be dyed – wish me luck!

4 September

Well. My hair is bright, bright white. At first it scared me somewhat, and I regretted it, but now I like it. I'm not sure how Caitlin will react, though. I chickened out of the cinema last night – unsettled by the hair and missing Caitlin. I made my poor friend Alison listen to me dithering over whether to phone the child or not. Eventually Tim came home and we really pushed the boat out by doing a middle-of-the-night shop at Sainsbury's. Oooh, the exciting things one can do when one is childless.

I have had a great day today organizing our house. Our bedroom and bathroom are now totally de-cluttered and look like a style magazine photo spread. It will probably last about twenty-four hours, but it makes me feel great at the moment. And the moment's what it's all about. Tonight we're going to the cinema. Going out on a Saturday night always reminds me of being fifteen. Fifteen was an excellent year for me. I looked great and I discovered sex and power. Tim, who knew me slightly, says I was a little intimidating. I remember being terribly shy and scared of other girls and their bitchiness. Boys, however, were great fun and would do pretty much anything I wanted them to – that mix of innocence and sexual power is very exhilarating. And then I developed a little more emotional maturity and things became harder. But Saturday nights were spent in the bathroom for hours, not being able to eat because I was nervous / excited and then out into the pubs and parks of Tunbridge Wells to snog and break up with an endless stream of boys.

I've got diaries from that period of my life and I'm not sure what I want to do with them. I have no idea what Caitlin will be like at that age – under normal circumstances a mother tells her daughter as much as she thinks appropriate at each stage, I guess. I shall just have to trust Tim and my parents to give her whatever information about me they want to. That is strange, the feeling that the 'me' left behind for her to know will be based on other people's memories. Except, of course, for this. Which is why I write so much – have always written so much. THIS IS ME.

Weeze and I were real cinema fanatics. There's something about sitting in the dark and being immersed in the projected world that is quite unlike any other experience. Although I work in the theatre and love it to pieces, if I'm totally honest – and don't tell anyone because I'll never work again – I prefer the cinema. I love the fact that it washes over me and absorbs me. I stop being a 'me' and am just part of 'it'. Weeze was the same, she loved the whole ritual of paying for the tickets, buying the popcorn and then entering the dark arena, not knowing if you'll come through the ensuing ordeal unscathed or changed for the rest of your life. Films can do that, they can change you, can make you weep and bawl. I have only ever cried once in the theatre, and weirdly enough it was during a critically panned show called *Hunting of the Snark* – it really affected me. But get me in the cinema, turn the lights down and nearly anything will set me off.

Weeze and I had a particularly turbulent month at the cinema when we went to see three harrowing films in a row, *The Piano*, *Schindler's List* and *Shadowlands* all in the space of a couple of weeks. Talk about crying. After *The Piano* Weeze and I went for a drive and didn't say a word for half an hour we were so stunned by the experience. After *Schindler's List* we both cried in the car in the car park for half an hour, holding each other, and after *Shadowlands* I couldn't leave the cinema for half an hour because I was wailing, as was Weeze, and in the end an usher came and asked us if we were all right.

I should just say two particular theatre practitioners have changed my life and because of them I went into theatre – Steven Berkoff and the French physical theatre genius Philippe Genty. They changed the way I perceived the world visually and creatively, and for that I am eternally grateful.

5 September

Caitlin returned and I wanted to squeeze her for hours. She was a little emotional about my blonde hair, but settled down very quickly. Two quotations I want to jot down. The first has been rattling around in my head for weeks and I've only just bothered to look it up exactly. It's from *Julius Caesar* and I wrote an 'O' level essay on it.

'Cowards die many times before their deaths;
The valiant never taste of death but once.
Of all the wonders that I yet have heard,
It seems to me most strange that men should fear;
Seeing that death, a necessary end,
Will come when it will come.'

I think of it whenever I find myself dwelling on my death. If for no other reason, Shakespeare should be taught because your subconscious is filled up with stuff like that. Stuff that does come back and mean things to you.

The other quotation is somewhat less high-flown. It's from *Harry Potter and the Philosopher's Stone* – a book everyone seems to be talking about, which I read over the weekend whilst Caitlin was away. These lines jumped out at me and comforted me:

'. . . love as powerful as your mother's leaves its own mark. Not a scar, no visible sign . . . To be loved so deeply, even though the person who loved us is gone, will give us some protection for ever. It is in your very skin.'

I'm there, in her, for ever.

6 September

First day back at school tomorrow. So this afternoon saw me in a shoe shop with dozens of other disorganized mothers, buying plimsolls and smart new school shoes. Then this evening I sewed on a few buttons and name-tapes, just for fun. I love doing all that mum stuff for her. These are the things which will be hard to relinquish later on, but for now I'm revelling in it.

The newspaper article came out today and was great (except for the lack of this exact website address) – the picture was very nice of all of us. Tim's bit made me feel all weepy, as all his writing does. When I write I sometimes kind of distance myself from my feelings, which makes them easier to deal with. When I read Tim's writing I feel it all over again through him. I wish I could make it all OK for him. That's what a life partnership is about partly. Still, we're squeezing the most out of the time at the moment. I want to give him every last drop of happiness there is in me.

8 September

I have had an extremely exciting day. The *Daily Mail* newspaper has asked me to do a weekly column! I will, of course, continue this diary because it is my own thing, but a weekly column in a national paper is a bit of a dream come true.

Other news today was Caitlin doing her first rehearsal in the theatre for Tim's *Oh What a Lovely War* – she was s-o-o-o sweet. She has a 'pretend acting Mummy' who leads her on to the stage, then she asks for a lollypop and sits and licks it whilst watching a song and dance act. Because it was only a rehearsal they didn't have a real lollypop and so she diligently mimed licking her hand for the full three minutes she was on stage. I was so proud of her. She's only in the first half, so I whisked her home to bed before the end of the show. Adrenalin from the *Daily Mail* thing is keeping me buzzing tonight. I caught myself thinking it was almost worth having cancer . . . Then I felt guilty. Still, in my heart I've always longed to be a writer and here I am . . . with something to write about.

Tomorrow my mother's taking me to Brighton to pick up my designer eye-patches – I can't wait to see them. I'm also going to show my mum the flat. We've had the survey done and it looks good, so that's all going ahead as planned. When I think of it I picture just walking out of the door and being on the beach in minutes. Beaches when they are empty, like in the winter, are so calming. It will be a refuge for whenever we need to stare out at the sea. A place we know we can escape to.

9 September

First night of the play tonight and Caitlin was fabulous. I was so proud I thought I would faint. She said a line! In front of an audience! I also went down to Brighton this afternoon to pick up my new eye-patches. They are great – different colours and materials – and one is a faux fur eye complete with huge false eyelashes. They are a bit tricky to fit my glasses over, so I'm definitely going to try and go for contact lenses.

My mum took Caitlin swimming and I wandered along the beach, gazing wistfully out to sea ... Or at least that's how I looked in my mind's eye. In the film of my life that often runs inside my head, parallel to my real life. In reality I was more blank than wistful. I think that's what's so relaxing about the sea, the sound of the waves is like a mantra – it washes away thoughts, leaving you just where you are. On the beach, gazing out to sea. I could do it for hours. The light is lovely there too – I felt like a solar panel being re-charged by the sun and the sea air. I really feel well at the moment. More than well, really. The cancer feels like a bonus card at the moment, giving me the opportunity and incentive to do things I would never otherwise have. I just want time now, time to enjoy this, to keep feeling like this for as long as possible.

11 September

I woke up on Friday morning feeling like death warmed up. Dizzy and sick and shivery. The only good thing is that last time I felt like this I thought I was dying, whereas this time I see it as a blip that I will recover from. I called my GP, Dr Thorpe, straight away and got some anti-sickness drugs and some antibiotics sorted out. They are going into me via a syringe driver, so it doesn't matter if I'm sick. I don't really feel well enough to write, but I thought I'd let you know why I'm absent. I will write again as soon as I feel up to it. Au revoir.

13 September

Well, I'm feeling a lot better. I'm taking it easy today, as Caitlin is in school anyway, but I've stopped being sick and feel much more cheerful. I've even decided I'm ready for autumn. Not the overcast days like today, but the crisp, frosty days with deep blue skies, where you go for crunchy walks in parks and can just see your breath hang for a moment in the air. It's clear skies that I love, not heat, and I think autumn is so exhilarating. I feel as though I'm in a sort of a lull at the moment. I feel generally very well, I haven't had any new symptoms for a while – if anything, with the taste buds and the balance, I've got a bit better. So there's a respite from the sense of urgency I often have, a chance to catch my breath and get on with being part of the living world. My main preoccupation this week will be Tim's birthday – it's on the 20th and after my amazing presents I want to do something just as wonderful for him. Also, Tim is organizing a week-long series of open house art exhibitions and art 'happenings' all around Tunbridge Wells, so that should keep us both busy for a while. I've finished the Harry Potter books by J. K. Rowling that I quoted last week – very enjoyable escapist fantasy stuff.

The 'Hijack Arts Festival' that I was organizing was basically set up to give Weeze an exhibition. I wanted her to

have her photos shown publicly and I knew that if I didn't organize it, it might take ages for her to find a gallery or a space that would accept her work. So I set up an entire festival with friends who are poets, artists, actors and musicians. It was to be a guerrilla festival, with works happening in and around the public without them being aware the festival was on, and it would be packed full of challenging work that would shock and surprise the general populous of our sleepy little town. Well, it would have done, had Weeze not got ill. This was really the turning point for her and it makes me sad to read her optimism about blips and thinking she was actually a little bit better, because within such a short period of time she would be too ill to do anything and this time there would be no reprieve.

14 September

I feel a lot better today. The performances of *Oh What a Lovely War* went brilliantly, incidentally. Caitlin received her own round of applause a couple of times and she got her line right each night: 'Can I have a lolly, please?' Tim said he could hear her back in the lighting box. I watched one night from the wings, then got ill and my mother had to take her to the other performances. Tim nearly exploded with pride each night. He's now a little flat after the excitement of the show. Still, he's got a big art festival thing to plan next. Life is a little surreal today, as the *Daily Mail* article came out. There were a few calls about TV interviews, but I'm happy with one column a week. I don't want street recognition. Hopefully the column won't affect our lives too much. In a way, though, I feel that life is so strange in my position anyway, that it would be much harder to carry on trying to live life as though nothing was happening.

Caitlin had her first full day at school yesterday – she stayed for lunch so that she could do ballet in the afternoon. S-o-o-o sweet. I picked her up and the first thing she said was, 'We didn't do pliés,' as though I had conned her by suggesting that they might. She had a great time, but was exhausted last night. I love the fact that she still comes into our bed in the middle of the night. It means I get an extra five or six hour cuddling time each day. I know we should probably have stopped it, but I think it's nice for all of us. And the bed's big enough. I'm going to try and get on top of Tim's birthday treats, now I'm feeling better. Pip, pip.

In fact the bed is bigger specifically for that reason. When Caitlin was little and used to come into bed it made very little difference to the actual space we had to lie in, but as she grew and took to lying horizontally across the mattress, Weeze and I found ourselves squeezed further and further towards the outer more uncomfortable inches of the bed. In the end it got beyond a joke, and when after the tenth day in a row I'd woken up unable to turn my head to the right because it was stuck that way, I decided enough was enough and that something had to be done. Weeze and I talked it over – either we took two or three nights of disturbed sleep to get Caitlin used to sleeping in her own bed all the way through the night, or we went out and bought the biggest bed we could find and tried to wean her out of it in her early teens. An hour later we had ordered a giant Gothic-style bed, and when it finally arrived we all slept like logs for months. Now, however, Caitlin wants to have physical contact with me all night when she comes in, so she chases me across the vast expanse of the bed with her razor sharp toenails, and when there's nowhere left to roll she's got me just where she wants me. At that point she strikes. For some reason she likes to plunge her feet in between my buttocks – maybe it's the warmth or something. As soon as she's scratched her way agonizingly into the crevice, she then does a series of rabbit kicks to get herself comfortable. It's lucky I love her so much or goodness knows what I'd do at these moments of excruciating pain.

When I go to bed, I go to bed alone. Caitlin doesn't come in until the early hours. Climbing into such a big bed on your own amplifies the pain of loss – it is impossible not to feeling lonely faced with so much acreage of cold white linen.

15 September

I got two very different responses to yesterday's article. One was from a very religious man who comes from a position of love, but gets angry because I do not believe that God is going to make me live. The other was a woman who lives near me who brought round a huge plate of Norwegian waffles and a card. It was such a non-judgemental expression of love and sympathy from a comparative stranger that it really bowled me over. The religious thing I find exhausting at the moment. I just don't feel like dealing with other people's emotions to do with my illness. Sometimes I'm up for a debate, but not now. I feel that we're dealing with it OK at the moment and that our family unit is strong and that I don't want to have to justify myself to anyone.

On a more positive note, I am going back to drama class

this evening. My main reason for stopping was that I was falling over and now that I have the eye-patch I don't, so I'm going to give it a go again. Tim was so lovely today. I came home from playing at a friend's house after school and there was a jewellery box on the kitchen table and in it was the most beautiful necklace and earrings from Tim. A present for being a proper writer and getting the *Daily Mail* job. It was so unexpected I welled up with tears and felt totally mushy. He's so lovely and I'm so lucky. I feel very close to Tim and Caitlin at the moment – a bit like we're going through all of this with the world on one level, through the writing, but that it's important to preserve us as a unit too. Lots of cuddles.

18 September

Sorry I haven't written for a few days. I woke up on Thursday feeling dreadful and being sick again – it happens so suddenly. This time it was decided that it could best be nipped in the bud if I came into the hospice for a couple of days, so I came in yesterday. And slept lots. This time, however, I have my computer with me – although there is some thought that writing is partly what I need a rest from. Perhaps I overdid it going to Drama on Wednesday evening – but I did enjoy it. It really takes me out of myself and makes my brain work in a different way. If I'm up to it I want to be in the Christmas show, which is a spoof of A *Christmas Carol*.

I have a lovely room again, with a garden view and a lot of interesting sky to look at – mainly blue with an ever-changing cloudscape to entertain me. Anyway, I don't feel like writing much, I just wanted to let you know why I haven't written – they're trying to get me out on Monday for Tim's birthday. I don't think we'll be doing anything too ambitious after all, but it will be good to be together and hopefully at least make it to the cinema or something.

Later

A bit down tonight. A new kind of pain, which is always a little worrying. Still, the staff here are brilliant. I've read a book that Tim brought in for me yesterday – a biography of Alexis Soyer, the chef who invented soup kitchens to feed the poor of London and Ireland and who did at least as much as Florence Nightingale to turn the Crimean War around. He was a marvellously flamboyant character. As well as caring for the nutrition of the destitute, he cooked the most extravagant dinners imaginable for Royalty. The menus from the mid-nineteenth century are quite unbelievable to the modern palate. He also wore all his clothes cut on the bias, *à la zouge zouge*, as he termed it, and loved the theatrical side of life. As well as his hundreds of inventions for the kitchen, he invented a trick suit which changed from morning to evening dress at the pull of a string and a device for rescuing people who have fallen through ice on lakes. The Victorians were so enthusiastic and full of ideas. There were so many 'gentleman' explorers and inventors. It must have been an exciting time to have been around, so many new things – photography and ballooning to name just two. Mind you, hell if you had no money, like most of the population. Still, at least Alexis Soyer was there dishing out his Christmas dinner for 22,000 of London's poorest.

19 September

In better spirits this morning. Last night I was a little low and couldn't sleep for a while. Writing helps, though, and I wrote a long letter to Caitlin, which got a lot of the sadness out of me. In the same way that it can feel as though tears relieve physical symptoms such as headaches, I feel that the release of emotions through talking and writing can, perhaps, relieve the pressure caused by the tumour.

A friend of mine, Val, brought me round a video of a documentary about Annie Leibovitz, which I have just watched. It was great – she's *brilliant* and it got me all fired up about pictures again. I have talked to my 'webmaster' Gavin and we shall put up my next gallery this week, once I'm on my feet again and out of here. Tim's going on a tour of Stamford Bridge (Chelsea Football Club's grounds) for his birthday treat, then home for a birthday tea with Caitlin and me and then we're going to the cinema. Nothing too exciting, but no point in exhausting myself, and he'll be pleased just to have me home. Thank you so much, everyone, for all the messages. There have been so many in the guest book since the *Daily Mail* article that I haven't been able to answer the majority of them – they are all hugely appreciated and mean a great deal to me. I can feel the love out there. Thanks.

So my last birthday with Weeze alive was spent looking round Chelsea Football Ground. I went up with a good friend and Weeze's webmaster, Gav, and we laughed loads, but overall I'd say it was the saddest birthday I can remember. Weeze came out of the hospice too quickly and should have had another few days to get fully recovered. As it was, she was so keen to get home for my birthday that she came out still weak and feeling rough. It was lovely to have her out and I appreciated the effort she'd gone to, but there was a large part of me that didn't want it to be my special day. I wanted life to go on as normal – special days only make you think about life and where you are, and who needs that. I knew this would be the last time I would hear Weeze say 'Happy Birthday, Tig', and kiss me and give me presents. I knew that the next time I had a birthday it would just be me and Caitlin, and I'd be alone and desperate for a hug from my beautiful wife. I don't want a birthday again without her, I want time to stop still. I think I'll stay at twenty-nine for a few years and when I feel somewhat healed I'll start again. I hated the melancholy that overtook me that day. I couldn't hide it from Weeze, and she'd gone to so much effort to organize things for me and get herself out of the hospice.

21 September

Well, I'm home and eating and trying to rest as much as possible. Tim's birthday was fine — it was nice to be home for it, but I am finding it hard to relax at the moment. I've been worried about Caitlin a little and her child-minding arrangements. But then again guilt is part and parcel of motherhood, as far as I can work out. I worry about spreading myself too thin and not having enough 'quality time' with Caitlin — that's fine if it's because I'm ill, but feels less fine if it's because I'm writing. I don't know, sometimes I just seem to have too much time to lie in bed and let worries chase themselves around my head. Patience, patience, rest, rest. Grrrr, it's frustrating. Still, much nicer to be home, where I feel I belong and have more of my life at my fingertips. Not much else to say at the moment and I don't want to write just for the sake of it, so take care out there. I may not write for a couple of days — don't worry, it's just that I want to have something to say . . .

23 September

I've got yet another infection, which is a pain, but I'm feeling OK. No dramatic highs or lows, just OK with where I am at the moment. I'm really pleased with the latest lot of pictures in gallery 3. I'm beginning to sort out what I'm doing for Tim's Highjack Arts Festival that he's running in Tunbridge Wells in November. I've decided to do a series of pictures about cancer rather than the sweet children stuff I've done before. Some from the hospice, some doctors and things, some self-portraits. It is very helpful for me to be concentrating on photography at the moment, so that I don't get swept along with the whole media thing and forget what it is that I have a real passion for. My writing fulfils one side of me, but it is very self-absorbed and introspective. My photography takes me out of myself and quite literally forces me to look and focus outside me.

I think pictures can be so much more powerful than words sometimes. I also thought I'd have a play on the computer at overlaying words and pictures to make images. If you haven't checked out the new gallery, look at Professor Gleeson's hands over my notes and my hand writing with the drip thing in the back of it. I don't want to go on about it and sound immodest, but I really like those pictures and they feel like they mean something. It's like I feel I am beginning to cross the line between nice family snaps and 'Art'. How pretentious, but I hope you see what I mean. Anyway, I'm off to get Caitlin from school, so bye.

24 September

I've just read the latest guest book entry, which made me feel a little strange. It says I'm terribly brave, but today I do not feel so brave. I think that bravery to me would be bearing my problems stoically, rather than splashing my feeling around the world. This is my way of pulling everyone along with me, so that I don't have to do it all alone. I went to see my sister Dee today – well, I actually spent most of the day on the M25 – but anyway, it was pretty exhausting. I think part of me wasn't ready to leave the Hospice in the Weald earlier this week. There is something so emotionally and physically comforting about the knowledge that someone is always on hand to talk and bring you tea and toast in bed.

When Caitlin had finally gone to bed (I think she is punishing me a little for having left her at the weekend – she's being quite hard work), Tim and I had a great chat about what I'm doing with my life. I worry that this whole cancer thing has taken over me so completely that I can't be part of normal conversation and life any more. But Tim was great, as he always is and I feel OK now. Not heroic, just OK. Tomorrow is a family day, with a birthday party to go to with Caitlin. Then I want to do some serious photography. And maybe some poetry...

25 September

Big long day. I went to a birthday party this afternoon and got lost in watching Caitlin. She went gradually from my lap to joining in all the games and dances. Watching the concentration on her face as she followed the movements of the 'entertainer' (I use this term in the loosest possible sense) – it was wonderful to watch and pulled me out of myself. Made me realize how I have removed from her a little recently. Probably just normal for the age, nothing to do with cancer and stuff, but we used to be almost painfully close. Telepathically in tune with emotions. I felt I entered her world properly today.

Came home completely drained. The tiredness that I feel at the moment is very extreme. I had a lie down before dinner and I was too tired to sleep or to move or to think. It was as though I just switched off. Then we ate and I had a cuddle and de-brief of the day with Tim, then decided to go to bed early-ish for me (10.30) to try to knock the tired, shaky feeling I've had all week on the head. I just dropped in here to read any new mail and guest books. And have filled up with tears after reading the last two on the guest book. I am so, so lucky. I know it sounds trite, but to feel the love and support from the world that I have – I am so grateful. Looking at the other mums at the party, I cannot feel worse off than them. I never wanted to be a housewife / mother anyway. Ever since having Caitlin, I have agonized on and off about 'fulfilling' myself and being creative. And I'm doing so much now. I shall go to sleep smiling tonight.

26 September

A really good day today. Each time I get over a shaky stage there is a huge sense of relief that it was just a phase, that I am not just shaky for good now. Today I didn't think or talk about being ill. Instead we went to Sainsbury's, had some good friends round for lunch and played in the sun in the park. Caitlin was in a good mood, I cooked well and all was right with the world. The priorities seemed right – family, food, friends – Sunday stuff.

Something that I got for Tim for his birthday was a 'survival weekend' in Wales for himself and a couple of friends. They are going to live on rabbits and in their own camp for three days the weekend after next. I thought it would be a good break from looking after Caitlin and me – and also good material for anecdotes ... he has been having fun buying knives and waterproof clothes and things, but I think it was probably a strange present, compared to the luxury he gave me. Mud versus manicure. One of the friends is vegetarian and not looking forward to living on food he has to skin – still, it will stand them in good stead should the millennium bug hit and everyone needs to survive on their wits. I'm still considering what exciting things Caitlin and I shall do for the weekend. She seems to have got over my stay in the hospice and has been lovely to me all day today. I'm sure she's picked up that I have felt much better too. I'm looking forward to doing some work this week whilst Caitlin is at school – itching for my camera at the moment. I hope the weather obliges me with some light. It is so wonderful when energy replaces tiredness, even in small doses.

28 September

Two steps forward, one step back. I woke up this morning with a splitting headache that morphine couldn't shift. Nothing for it but to sleep all day, much to my frustration. It was my own fault, as I stayed up until one in the morning the night before, after a couple of days of entertaining and shopping and cooking and general life. I get so cross at the moment that my body can't keep up with what I see as perfectly modest demands.

There are women of my age who go out to night clubs

and stay up dancing all night and go to work the next day. There are people who manage to look after eight children. And my body physically shakes if I push Caitlin's pushchair uphill across our little park. I get short of breath if I bring Tim a cup of tea to his office on the top floor of our house. So I live through my mind and my eye instead. My body is unreliable, so I project myself out. My sight is the way I experience the world. On days like today when I am in bed all day, I live in amongst the clouds outside the window – or the clouds painted on to our ceiling. Perhaps if I spent the time I could bring my body up to a better level of fitness, but I lose patience with it. My mother gave me a lovely foot massage this afternoon, but the pleasure was more about the love transferring from mother to daughter than about feet.

Tomorrow morning a spiritual healer is coming here. He got in touch after the article in the newspaper and phoned at a time when my resistance was low and as he was very insistent and said he was in the area anyway, I accepted his offer. He is not expecting a cure, apparently, but hopes to relieve any symptoms I might be experiencing at the time. I'm sure it's terribly unfair of me, but I feel very defensive about healing. I suppose I feel that most of the time Tim and I know where we are with this disease and we are dealing with that. To open yourself up to other possibilities and think about hope is tiring. Anyway, I'm not expecting anything tomorrow, but I shall let you know what happens.

29 September

I wish the healer had done something about the weather. The weather has such a direct effect on my mood, more than anything else. I also hope it cheers up for Tim's weekend in

Wales. The healer was nice and I felt bad for feeling so resistant to the idea of him. It is hard, though, because there is still that little part of me that wants to say 'Oooh, can you make it all go away?' And most of the time I'm so focused on the good that I can see in the illness and the way I'm dealing with it that I don't want to hear that little voice that just wants it all to go away. Still, it was a relaxing half-hour's meditation and he wasn't promising anything, so there was nothing to be lost. And he did drive a long way to come and see me, which was sweet of him.

This greyness and rain, though. Today I'm not in pain, really, just sitting around. I wonder what I would be doing today if I didn't have cancer. Caitlin at school. Would I be hoovering up or making a cake for tea or sitting around with some other mothers talking about kitchen decorations? Am I lucky to have a purpose to the majority of my days, a sense of urgency that is lacking from most people's lives? I don't know ... This afternoon I'm going to do something lovely and crafty or cookingy or something with Caitlin and put the heating on and snuggle. Tim's out teaching drama and my mum's here to keep us company – three generations of girls. In America perhaps we'd be quilting ...

30 September

Dizzy today. Tim has gone out to the cinema and I decided to stay in so as to conserve my energy. Then we had a chat and came to an important decision. This last week or so I have been taking it easy so I don't burn myself out. However, I can see a point in the not-too-distant future when I might not be able to overdo it in the first place. So we're going to take calculated risks and have days out, budgeting in days in bed afterwards. For a start, we thought we might take Caitlin out of school for a day every couple of weeks and do terribly exciting things like go to shows in London and go to Paris on the train. We were watching the Disney film of the *Hunchback of Notre Dame* this evening and thought it would be great to just whisk her off there. And at this age it makes no difference if she misses the odd day of school.

I'm getting withdrawal symptoms for fun at the moment. I feel grotty and tired a lot but I also want to have FUN. Tonight I felt jealous of Tim's health for the first time ever, I think. I shoved him out of the house to the cinema – Caitlin was asleep and I'm OK, so there's no reason for him to be stuck here, but I just had this pang of jealousy. He's so fit and young and strong and could go dancing or anything . . . I can dance for about half a song before collapsing. The jealousy has faded into a wistful pang now – I suppose it is surprising that it's the first time I've felt it. Maybe that's why I got him the survival weekend – I want to put his body through its paces as I can't push mine! I used to enjoy pushing my body through yoga and T'ai Chi. I shall go and do a few gentle stretches now to feel I have some control over my body.

Chapter 10

━━

2 October

The last two days have been a blur of being sick and in pain.
I go up and down so quickly – it is so disconcerting for all of
us. This morning I was on track for going back into the hospice,
then, after a new combination of drugs in two different syringe
drivers, I'm at least sitting up in bed. I had a very symbolic
dream at lunchtime. I was with lots of very ill people who
had body paint all over them. In order to get better, they
had to have the paint washed off. I was in agony, but couldn't
get better, because there was nothing to wash off. Then, at
the end of the dream, the paint appeared and I knew I would
get over this latest infection. I woke up wanting a cup of tea,
knowing I had turned the corner.

3 October

The sky is blue, there is a soft breeze, I'm not being sick, life ain't so bad. Caitlin and I had a lovely morning reading in bed ... My two older sisters, Dee and Jan, are coming down to stay next weekend when Tim is on his survival weekend. They are lovely and will help out with Caitlin and me and make Tim feel happy about going. This afternoon Tim's brother and family are coming to see us – Tim's taken Caitlin out now to re-stock the house with food. The girls all get on very well. I'm still amazed at the difference in how I feel. On Friday I was so ill I have almost no recollection of who came to see me in terms of doctors and nurses ... today I feel human again – getting Caitlin to count with me, worrying about stupid things like clean school uniforms.

Goals for this week are to go to the cinema (*American Pie* – silly and funny-looking) and to get enough rest that I definitely won't be ill for Tim's weekend away. As soon as the pain goes and I can see beyond the illness, I feel so much lighter all over. I can see through the clouds literally and metaphorically today. Pain is so debilitating, it obliterates all else – without it I am me again.

Later

I find myself returning mentally again and again to when I was fifteen. Perhaps because that was when I really started writing. Similar kinds of writing to this, really. I often think that this is just an extension of teenage angst; it is only because I am a bit older and have a terminal illness that people think this has something more profound in it than your average teenage ramblings ... When you are a teenager you have more time. Time spent listening to records in your room, time spent lying on your bed staring at the ceiling, trying to figure out who you are, what is important, what you believe in . . . Then you get busy, with much of it still unresolved, life gets on with you, responsibilities happen and unless you are a writer or something, the ceiling staring time stops.

I've got that teenage time back, and to one who used to write poetry at fifteen the combination of time and a laptop computer could hardly fail to result in this website.

I always said that if I had another life, if I hadn't met Tim, basically, I would have chosen one with a more monastic bent. I only spent a very brief time in the Buddhist monastery where I went on retreat, but I TOTALLY 'got' it. The mental freedom afforded by strict routine and solitude was very seductive . . .

I have been dipping into *The Penguin Book of Diaries* and came across Katherine Mansfield's. She died of TB at thirty-five and she wrote beautifully:

'In the evening, for the first time for – I felt rested. I sat up in bed and discovered I was singing within. Even the sound of the wind is different. It is joyful, not ominous. And black dark looks in at the window and is only the black dark.'

I shall end on that happy note tonight. Discovered I was singing within. Lovely.

4 October

Nice evening with Caitlin. I have started cooking with her a lot more – letting her have more responsibility so that she can be more involved with things with me. So tonight she chopped the courgettes for the lasagne with a proper knife. She really felt that she helped me. I've also started giving her candle-lit baths in the evening. I love the light of candles and I think it is a really good multi-sense memory to build up. That sounds so clinical, doesn't it? I just mean she can always have candle-lit bubble baths and remember me. They help me when I'm sad.

There is a documentary series that has just started on TV here which is about a family who are living life as they would have a hundred years ago. It is strange because I was going to volunteer us for it when I got ill. The candle thing reminded me of it. It is like the monastic thing too, I think. Not that you would have much time doing all the housework and things of a hundred years ago, but there is a certain meditation in hard work. It is the opposite of what most people seem to strive for – more choice and more leisure time seem to be what we are supposed to want, but I don't know if it makes us any happier.

This evening I am happy, anyway, in a quiet sort of way. Happy to feel better and to appreciate Caitlin. I caught up on some boring paperwork – finally sorted our wills out and renewed the car insurance and mundane things like that. My mind is always clearer when there is nothing hanging over me. It would be clearer still without a bloody great bit of extraneous tissue clogging up the works, but one can't have everything in life!

Weeze loved to luxuriate in a bath, and she wanted to pass this memory of water and candles and oils on to Caitlin. She created a world of calm in our bathroom: the sweet smell of the soap, the way she swept her hair back from her face when it was wet, the way she rested her head back on the enamel with her eyes closed, blind eyes pointing towards heaven. It was all too much for me, it was too calm, too peaceful. She loved to be read to all the time, especially when she was in the bath, but I just couldn't do it. The nearer we got to her death, even if I didn't know when that would be consciously, the less able I was to see her at peace. In the candle light she was too magical, too serene – I couldn't cope with it, it made me want to cry. I just wanted to scream. The only sound in the room – that of the gently lapping water against her skin – was deafening, and I wanted noise, music, distraction. I needed to be shouting and dancing, or watching crap meaningless telly. Sitting in the bathroom with her speaking in hushed tones was too intense. It sucked me down into a melancholy which I found it hard to shake off. So it became her ritual, or hers and Caitlin's. I would stay downstairs and watch Chelsea lose to some crappy team or other, shouting at the screen, waving my fists helplessly, and Weeze would lie in the bath, think and calm her mind for the impending departure. I spend as little time in the bathroom now as I possibly can: I bathe Caitlin in the bath and tickle her and play loud games and then whisk her into a towel and off to bed, or I jump in the shower in the morning and try desperately to wash myself without thinking lest the melancholy should come again and a thousand other pictures and memories should overcome me.

5 October

Indigestion. How ridiculous and petty seeming, and yet how painful. That and a cold – I assume, as Tim and Caitlin have colds. I'm on so many drugs I doubt if any real symptoms can show their faces. Instead, I am dizzy, depressed and tired. I slept pretty much all afternoon, before waking up to do a little painting with Caitlin, then bathed her and put her to sleep. She was almost too good and beautiful tonight. There are times when I just feel so sorry for her, that she has to suffer any pain in her life. She is so perfect ... I'm sure I'm buying into the Victorian myth of the innocence of childhood, but it does sometimes feel as though she is a glass doll that I'm just waiting to drop. Hmmmm ... antibiotics make one depressed, I believe. That last remark should probably be struck from the record to save you all crying, but the record is here for better or worse, so I shall leave it in. My taste buds have reverted to their erstwhile dislike of sweets, perhaps it's just the cold. Just when I could do with some chocolate, too. At least you know I'll probably be back up again tomorrow – I'm nothing if not consistently inconsistent! Sleep well, all.

7 October

A bad headache yesterday, so more morphine and I slept pretty much all day. I am determined to let Tim go off tomorrow for his survival weekend, as I think he could really do with the break from responsibility. So, I am conserving as much energy as possible. My sister Janice will be here tomorrow afternoon, then my other sister Dee is coming on Saturday. I hope I'm well enough to enjoy some time with them, rather than just being looked after. I feel so sorry for people who don't have family to call on at times of crisis – I know that Dee and Jan would always drop everything to come and help us. It is a nice secure feeling that so many people do not have.

I feel mentally stronger than the last time I wrote – having made the decision that I WILL be well enough to let Tim go away feels good. Back in control a little ...

What do you do when the person you love starts sleeping all day long? You get up in the morning and you try not to wake them because you know that if you do they'll more than likely be sick. You dress your little girl and take her to school, and then you return home. You sit downstairs and drink tea, do a little shopping and then go up to her room and gently whisper in her ear. 'Weeze? Weeze, darling, do you want anything? A drink? Anything at all?' She rolls over and very quietly moans and says, 'No. Just want to sleep, feel sick.' So you leave her and you go downstairs again and you wait and wait. You could do some writing or read, but you find yourself numb and sad. The minutes and hours pass and you go to pick up your little girl. You laugh with the teachers and try to regain some sense of normality and fun, but you know that within seconds you'll be back in the house where your wife is lying asleep upstairs. The line of communication that you've always had has been removed. You can't wake her and tell her you feel bad. You have to ride out the day, get to the night and then crawl into the bed next to her and lie awake praying that tomorrow will be one of the good days when she wakes up feeling refreshed and alive. Then you hear a squeak from the other room and your little girl cries out 'Mummy, Mummy . . .', as she has done every night since she could speak, and you get out of bed, pick her up in your arms, take her into your bed and hold her close to you like a hot water bottle for soul comfort.

8 October

I'm feeling terribly soppy and missing Tim, even though he's only been gone about two hours! A little bit of me suddenly said, 'You've got limited time with your love and you've chucked him out into the rain!!?? Are you crazy?' But then I think that this will be one of the few times he will actually be able to concentrate on himself, not on looking after us all the time.

There are birthday presents and there are birthday presents. Being sent by your wife with your brother, father and two best friends away into the first chill of winter to an inhospitable part of the British Isles with the rain drizzling down, no food, no shelter and no home comforts could seem to be a cruel joke or something. But actually it was a gas. We drove most of the day to arrive in early evening at this cold, damp pub in a village in the Brecon Beacons that looked as if it could have been the set for a Hammer House of Horror movie. There we met Ginge, a sixty-year-old ex-SAS soldier who's travelled the world, met thousands of interesting people and killed them.

After we watched him sink pint after pint we were given a brief chat about safety and then, when the pub closed and we were all thinking we'd head upstairs for the night and start out first thing, we found out it wasn't time for bed, but time for a four-mile hike in the pitch black night, across rocky moors and bogs. Torches, apparently, are not allowed as they would give us 'torch blindness'. We were assured that our eyes would acclimatize much quicker to the dark without aid of artificial light. Well, an hour or so later, I was soaked and covered in mud and couldn't

232

see a sodding thing, when Ginge informed us we'd arrived at our destination. We were led to an old knackered tent and left there to get comfy. It was wet, cold and muddy and I must have managed to sleep for all of twenty minutes. It might have been more had I not been the last person in our group to fall asleep, and was kept awake by the snoring, moaning and farting of my family and friends.

For the next three days we walked, we learnt about the wilderness, we jumped into icy cold pools naked, we traversed freezing fast-flowing rivers, we made camp and I ate a can of tuna I'd smuggled into my backpack. More than anything, though, I enjoyed being there with this group of people who would be there with me after Weeze had died. It was a time for me to get to know my brother again, and we talked as we walked and all I wanted him to do was to hold me. As a child I idolized my big brother, and still do. I'm not sure why, but he reminds of a bear. A big cuddly bear, strong and loving. Owen and Gavin are like my other brothers, closer than friends and like rocks, steady and supporting. My dad, is my dad. He's my best friend, confidant and father. I love them all so much. When the weekend finished, I felt refreshed and renewed and ready to be there again, and as it turned out this would be my last opportunity to take such a break before Weeze died.

9 October

I feel much better about Tim being away today. I had been really worried about looking after Caitlin — more about her picking up on my lack of confidence than anything, I think. In actual fact it is going fine, and I have got more energy than I thought I would have, as well as plenty of support. I think it is so good for both Tim and me to know that he is not carrying the whole family on his shoulders all the time. He phoned last night from a pub where the course starts, telling me how hard-core it all is. The guy running it is ex-SAS and started the talk by telling them how life is all about survival – including emotional survival. He then went on to explain how his wife had died of cancer! So it goes on – you can't get away from it. Tim said they were going for a freezing cold river swim this morning. I've just put the heating on to get cosier! My sisters are both here now, with my nephew Harry, whom Caitlin idolizes.

12 October

Just a quick entry in case anyone is worried. Tim survived his weekend and, barring our car needing towing back from Wales, it went really well and was definitely a good thing to have done. Much male bonding and wading through freezing rivers. I had a good day on Sunday, but then a dreadful day yesterday. I seem to get sick as soon as I cut down the steroids at all – even if just from a syringe driver to taking them orally. The steroids are anti-inflammatory and without them I have extremely bad headaches and sickness. I also have another infection. Yesterday I felt – not scared – but that the disease was out of my control. I suppose that is silly, it never was within my control, but most of the time before (and today again) I felt in control of my reactions to it. Yesterday I felt a very definite 'I'm not ready to be quite this ill' feeling. Tim suggested some kind of vitamin programme to keep up quality of life and I think he's right.

13 October

Right. A get-off-your-bum-and-sort-your-attitude-out day. (Me, that is, not you. I'm sure your attitude is fine.) I got up this morning and had a great talk to Tim and got the necessary oomph to get out of bed and try to get on top of things. I have an appointment with Professor Gleeson on Friday, so maybe he'll have some new drug suggestions or something. Talking about symptoms and drugs is so boring, but it is what is preoccupying me at the moment. That is probably why I've been so down – the physical limitations have been really pushing themselves at me, getting in the way of the mental stuff. It is hard to get a rounded perspective on life when one is horizontal in bed.

On a lighter note, we have some gorgeous curtains in our bedroom now. They go perfectly with the walls and the cloud effects and mean that Caitlin has stopped waking up quite so early – thus giving Tim that extra little bit of time in bed.

15 October

This entry is a bit of an apology to all the people who have been emailing me for the last few days – I haven't been feeling terribly positive (I'm sure you've noticed . . .) and haven't felt like writing much. You have all been so supportive always, and I know so many people check into this website every day to see what I have written and this last week I feel I have hit a really low point. I think that this is largely medication-related. This morning I had a good meeting with my surgeon at Guy's and he advised coming off my antibiotics, as my infections seem to have cleared up – this may well help, as they have a depressing effect. Otherwise, I've just got the blues, I think. It was bound to happen at some point, and at least there is one thing that is certain, that I can hold on to: ALL THINGS PASS. This is so true. You cannot stay sad for ever. And I am not completely sad. I can still see happiness in things and I can see that this feeling will pass.

It is all very well feeling positive when one feels well, as I've said before, but when one feels ill it is harder. And I do feel ill a great deal of the time at the moment.

Ten minutes later . . .

I am the Queen of Mood Swings . . . my gorgeous husband has just given me a pep talk and I feel 100 per cent better. We are going to the cinema for an early showing of the comedy *American Pie*, then I'm going to dye my hair red. Tomorrow I shall buy a load of face-packs and stuff for the spots (bloody steroids) on my face and also some high-necked tops. My mood has not been helped by the steroids making me feel ugly. I feel loads more positive and felt I should let you know after that last miserable entry . . . I'm off to the cinema!

16 October

I feel s-o-o-o-o much better today. It is as though I am suddenly 'me' again. I have had a lovely family day, and everything seems to be right. It is as though I am back in tune with the universe. You know when things just seem to fit, to be right. Lights change at the right time, there are parking spaces where you want them, that kind of thing. It is all about trust, I think. I feel today as though I have been standing, hovering on the edge of a ravine, swathed in mist. For the last couple of weeks I have been clinging to the edge, not daring to do anything. Today I relaxed and felt as though I did a swan-dive into the mist. Life will be what it will be and I trust that it is right. Whatever happens.

On a practical level, coming off antibiotics may have helped and I dyed my hair red last night. I feel much happier and more 'me' with darker hair. It really is amazing how different I feel. Today I have felt truly relaxed and happy. And able to laugh again at the cancer and to feel light-hearted. I bought a book today of Katherine Mansfield's short stories and in one, 'Bliss', the lead character talks of feeling 'as though you'd suddenly swallowed a bright piece of that late afternoon sun and it burned in your bosom, sending out a little shower of sparks into every particle, into every finger and toe . . .' The book just fell open there and it was the first thing I read. My heart soared and everything just felt right. The relief is huge, as well. There is a fear that I have sometimes, that when I get down, I will be down for ever, that I am just ill now and will never be happy again. I know really that all things pass, as I said yesterday, but it is such a relief to have my sense of humour and fun back, to feel myself again. Sleep well, my friends.

18 October

A very exciting meeting this afternoon. A lovely lady from HarperCollins came down and wants Tim and me to write a book! I thought at first she would want it to be a posthumous book – after all, it is the logical ending of this diary – but no, it is to be a life-affirming book about all sorts of things, not just dying of cancer. It is all so exciting. I have always wanted to go into a bookshop and see a book of mine there. And Tim and me doing one together is lovely. It means discipline and deadlines and things, but I'm sure we can do it. Tim works far better with a deadline in view anyway. Although these things are tiring, they are also the kinds of things that keep one alive, I'm sure. The incentive of attending a book launch will be worth a truckload of steroids, I'm sure.

21 October

Up and down, up and down. Another couple of days in bed. I'm not a terribly reliable diarist, I'm afraid. Feel free to check in once a week, as opposed to daily . . . I feel generally pretty ill at the moment, but hopefully it's another blip. I had a good weekend, anyway, and if I take it really easily over the next few days, hopefully I'll have a good week next week. I have been thinking about an au pair or nanny or something. Just to take the pressure off Tim, really. I'm just not up to being alone with Caitlin at all at the moment – partly because I keep walking into walls! That might get better, but in the meantime it makes me feel very unstable. It would also take some of the pressure off my mother – she is spending most of her time here, when she's not at work, and I feel bad asking her to do so much. She is wonderful, though, and Caitlin adores her.

At the moment I feel as though I am 'getting through' each day – it's a plus when I'm up and not sick . . . this diary helps me, as I can re-read past entries and see that I was well just a short time ago – I was writing about bliss just five days ago. That is helpful, as the mind is a tricky character and quite capable of convincing one that bleakness has been there for ever. I don't mean to sound too depressed: I'm not, I'm just physically low again and it feels as though I can't get a stretch of 'well' days. Still, slowly does it – I'm still off antibiotics and down to one syringe driver. Next week the plan is to come off the other. I shall write again when I have something to report.

22 October

A better day. I'm sorry to write entries like yesterday's. Today some good friends came round and brought a take-away. We also sorted out a bit more of a regular rota system of support. I also realized that I need to live much more in the moment and not worry about the future. It is true that the future is completely unpredictable, in all sorts of ways. I know that that is obvious and also impossibly trite – 'don't worry about the future' – but it is also true and if I spent all the time preoccu-pied with things to come then the things I can do now will pass me by. I think my mind has just been catching up with my body recently: my body has got iller and so my mind has needed a chance to adjust. It would be unreal if I was happy all the time – but I am happy more often than has come across in this lately I think.

25 October

The first time I have actually 'felt' like writing in a long time. I'm adjusting, I think, to living within new parameters. I'm going to take it much easier on myself. I'm afraid that means not answering emails (not that I've been doing much of that any-way). I'm only going to write this when I want to. And I'm going to grab all the beautiful moments I have left to me. Tonight the clouds at sunset are truly breathtaking and I feel lifted out of myself to see them. I can now admit that I need help and support – that my 'job' on this planet is not to die nobly or well, it is just to be and nothing more. I was putting myself under a lot of pressure to do this thing 'right', but there is no right or wrong. I am living as much as I can, but there is no rule book. I love the world, and it makes me sad to see my limitations creeping up on me. That is all. Grab a glass of wine and drink to the sun breaking through the clouds.

Later

I think that today I've kind of accepted that I'm going to die, on a different level. There are many levels of acceptance, and I'm sure I'll feel these transition times again, but for now, I feel I've come a stage further. And I feel some relief this evening, strangely enough, admitting it. I am that bit more ill. But I can live at this level for a long time. And by changing my expectations of what my life 'should' be like, I feel better. I've had an offer from an old friend to come and nanny for a month . . . I've discovered that (which I knew really) people are desperate to help and to listen, but I just needed to ask, and that in the past I was doing such a good job of coping that it was daunting. Things happen according to their proper time and place and now is the time for all good men to come to the aid of the party . . . speaking of parties, I'm planning on a humdinger of a Christmas and also Caitlin's got her fourth birthday in a month . . . calmer than for weeks, goodnight . . . xxxxxxxxxxx

27 October

I completely forgot to mention that on Saturday Tim and I took Caitlin to a story-telling day at our local theatre and saw a guy called Ben Haggarty. I wanted to thank him for bringing me some magic. Some wonderful, childhood magic. His stories were full of witches and magical beasts and just magic. And it was wonderful. It really took me out of myself and into another realm, where there is magic. I don't know why it was so important, but it was. He was great and I got a great deal from the day.

Otherwise I have been well for a couple of days in a row now (Whoopeee!) and am feeling OK. I still feel the need to talk a lot and to ask people to be around and to be supportive (whatever that means, exactly). Talking helps me a lot. We've been talking about Caitlin's birthday party, and a friend is going to help with that – we shall hire a local hall, I think. My parents want to do a big family Christmas at their house and have as many people around as possible, which is great and takes any pressure off us. I'm not scared of dying – or even of being ill – but I am worried about being alone at the moment. I feel the need for people around – for all of us to have breaks, especially Tim. I think that it is hard for us to think of exactly the kind of help that we need, in the same way as it is hard for people to know what to offer. On a practical level, Caitlin is not very keen on leaving us, even for an afternoon, at the moment, so that makes that kind of help tricky. She tends to think that I should either be asleep or actively playing with her, which is pretty exhausting. I'm probably just whingeing because it's half-term, and all will be easier next week!

2 November

Sorry I haven't written for so long. As you may have guessed, I'm in the hospice. I have been extremely dizzy since Thursday, and on Friday I passed out briefly, so we all thought it was best if I came in for a while to get a really good rest.

I have been in for a few days, during which time we have made some decisions. The really big one that my mother has made is to take some compassionate leave from work and help us in the house. It is a HUGE weight off my mind and will help Tim loads. At the moment I am pretty bedridden, so we need lots of help and Caitlin adores my mum (and she her, of course).

Caitlin got upset about this last change in routine. Since going back to school and having a lot of cuddles and reassurance from Tim, she has started sleeping again and so, in turn, has Tim. The house got pretty fraught for a few days, but is, I think, getting back on track. Easy for me to say from in here! I'm sleeping a lot and trying to eat and relax. At the moment the TV is on and Dame Thora Hird is advertising a reclining chair – the same type as is next to the bed. Because, after all, none of us is getting any younger . . .

I feel bad about not updating this earlier, but I was too ill. I hope I can remember how to do a new month from in the hospice.

3 November

> And now it is time
> (The Walrus said)
> To click those ruby heels.
> Leave this world of nonsense . . .
> There's no place like home . . .
> (A cancer-free one would be nice)

OK, God. I'm bored of this now. I'm learning my lessons – albeit begrudgingly, and I would now like a break, please. I am cutting back on all my 'ought to's' and feel far more in control of my life. I want to live for myself, for my relationships. I know I've said all this before, but it is really time now to live each day exactly how I wish it. So. No more deadlines for the *Daily Mail* (who have been wonderful), no more any obligations to others. I shall write this as and when I feel like it. I'm sorry for those of you who have been following this site daily for months – I shall keep it up in some form for as long as I can.

So. The plan is to leave here on Monday 8th, but probably bedridden and with a wheelchair for the odd outing to the park. I also feel that I've written so much about the way I've been feeling – now I just want to put down a load of stuff about me and my memories. I feel the diary has got a bit introverted (ha – a bit!) and maudlin of late.

I wrote this on Tuesday:

There is beauty wherever there is light falling, wherever there are shadows to balance it. The drop of pure white cream running down the side of a silver-dark jug has a simple beauty. The light and shade of folds of cloth on my bed. The hundreds of shades of light reflected throughout a jug and glass of iced water, dewy condensation on the sides.

Sunsets are never the same, yet always the most wonderful ever. The world is made up of light and shade and I could watch it for ever, for always, for as long as I have left. I feel myself retreating inwards – perhaps only temporarily – but retreating inwards from the world still. I want to gaze out of the window at the light on the trees, leaves, fields, the folds in the blanket over my knee. No longer bored of not-doing, content to be being.

I want to thank everyone s-o-o-o much for all the emails and support. And apologize for not replying, but I do need to be 'selfish' at the moment.

10 November

Hi there all, Tim here. Weeze wanted me to write a quick entry to tell you all what's been happening over the last few days. Having fixed up our bedroom with all the mod cons, TV, stereo, commode, video, incense burner, etc. I went in to pick Weeze up from the hospice on Monday. She is very weak and had considerable difficulty getting from her wheel-chair into the car and then even more problems getting from the car up the stairs and into bed. Anyway we made it and there she lies. She had a good Monday night, watched a couple of vids with me and Caitlin and chatted away until quite late. However, this seems to have taken it out of her and she's spent the last day and a half asleep, occasionally waking for some food, but nothing else. She's a different lady to the one that went into the hospice two weeks ago – tired, bedridden and now entirely dependent on others for everything. She appears to be out of pain and quite at peace which is about as much as I think we can hope for from now on. If she feels up to it I'm sure she'll be adding more entries but for now I'll add the odd bit, just to keep you all posted. These are hard dark days with tears never far from the surface.

15 November

So: what does it feel like? It feels like on one hand I ought to be struggling more: fighting death. I feel guilty about that, for Tim and Caitlin. I'm not drinking super-sweetened water and pushing back each wave of death. On the other hand there is the feeling that this is so right – choreographed almost, with everyone here. All my family are here and I have managed to say everything I ever wanted to say to everyone. I want to thank all of you so much. You have all given me a HUGE amount, just by listening, by letting me feel so much love. Thank you. It really has been a wonderful thing that you've done. The gift of listening is wonderful. It may feel to you as if I have done something, but really you have allowed me the chance to express myself written and photographically to the world. Thank You World.

20 November

Hello.

From the last entry it may be assumed that I am no longer here. Actually I am. I thought everything was wrapped up and felt I was dying. Since then my 'golden bird' has returned and although I am still dizzy and bedridden, I am not imminently dying. My family and friends are still here. Gavin, my webmaster, has been updating this.

Chapter 11

I'm now late on the deadline for the book. I was doing really well, writing every day, hitting my targets, but then I got to this bit of the book and I wanted to stop. Truth be told, I didn't want to write at all. I contemplated just leaving the book where Weeze left her diary, on an upbeat exclamation mark, but that would be cowardly and now I have to face telling you about her last three months in my own words as she stopped writing altogether.

I've taken up painting, large-scale abstracts. They're full of energy and dark movement and it's obvious to me that I've been trying to get something out of me, something that I was afraid to put down in words. I've never painted before in my life and I've found it incredibly liberating and therapeutic to work in a new medium. The paintings aren't great, but they're from somewhere very deep inside me and I think needed to come out. They've also been a wonderful focus away from writing the book, but now I've put down my brushes, stopped stretching any new canvases and think it's time I worked on finishing this picture and hopefully, by finishing it, to reach some kind of peace. How long or short this part will be, I'm not sure, I'm not going to plan it. I'll just write what comes into my mind and if it's too painful you may never know about it, but all I can promise is that I will try to be as true to the experience as I can be. I won't gloss over anything, I won't make it prettier than it was. So let's have a go and see where we get to by the end.

Shortly after her last entry, Weeze took to her bed again. She was dizzier than she'd ever been before and couldn't bear to open her eyes – the whole world would spin and spin. Consequently she chose to sleep. In sleep she was free, vaguely pain free and away from her body's frailties. She would get up occasionally, come downstairs, chat a little, have a kiss and then head for bed again. I took over full-time care of Caitlin and our lives turned inwards. We didn't go anywhere, people came to us. The outside world slowly disappeared and all there was was feeding Caitlin, feeding Weeze and trying to keep the house on an even keel. It was a phase that would last for the next three months and one which I found very difficult to snap out of when the whole thing was over.

One morning while Caitlin was at school, I was in the living room tidying up and Weeze was in bed asleep. I heard her stir and make her way down the corridor towards the bathroom. There was a loud thump. I stood still and waited for another noise and then heard a little voice, 'Tim, Tim could you help me.' I walked calmly up the stairs to find her collapsed at the foot of the short flight of stairs that leads into our bathroom. Weeze looked dazed and upset.

'I'm not sure what happened. I think I blacked out and fell down the stairs.'

'Are you OK, anything broken?'

She checked herself and said she felt OK, but a bit weird in the head. She started to cry and I tried to hold her but she gently pushed me away and looked ashamed.

'I can't bear it, I've wet myself. I'm so sorry, Tim.'

I helped her up and took her into the bathroom, I washed her, changed her clothes and then helped her back to bed. I then went back to clean up the carpet. It wasn't bad, it wasn't anything really, it was just what had to be done. I felt sorry for her, she was mortified by it. It was the lack of dignity that went with the whole experience. I went back to her and held her tightly. It was the start of the end and both of us knew it. After that fall nothing would be the same. I called the doctor and told him about her blacking out. She was back in the hospice within the hour. This was her last visit to the hospice.

It wasn't like the other trips to the hospice. Every other time she'd been in she'd stayed there for a few days, got herself well and truly rested and then came out, back on fighting form. This time she went in feeling ill and got progressively more ill. She was told within a day or so that she was unlikely to ever walk again – they believed the tumour had grown through her balance centre and that this wouldn't get better. As she told me, I found that tears were running down my face and I wasn't even conscious of crying. I held her hand and kept saying over and over again, 'It'll be all right, little one, it'll be all right.' They raised her drugs and gave her two syringe drivers which pumped her full of anti-sickness, pain-relieving drugs, as well as steroids and some other bits and pieces just for good measure. But this time they didn't seem to have much of an effect, she was being sick regularly and having great trouble keeping anything inside her. She also felt lonely and depressed in there. Before, she'd enjoyed the attention and care that the hospice gave her, but knowing that this was the last stage and that she might die soon she just wanted to be home, with her own things around her and her family there all the time. After a week or so and no improvement, we made the decision to bring her home – no one said to die, but everyone thought it.

The difference in the person that I'd taken into the hospice a week before and the person that I had to carry up the stairs a week later was horrific. She'd lost weight and most of her strength. But she was happy, happier than I'd seen her for a long time. That night the whole family sat round on our bed and chatted. She laughed and joked, and we were all convinced that things weren't as bad as they might be. That was that night, everything was different the next morning. Weeze couldn't wake up, she was too tired, exhausted beyond belief. That whole day went by without her eating or drinking, as did the next, and the next, and the next. The district nurses came in and told us that we had to get some water into her, so we took it in shifts to sit with her and give her water. At first she would sit up and sip a little but then even that became too much and we had to dip little sponges on a stick into water and then place that into her mouth for her to suck the tiniest amount of water from.

Things got worse and worse and the mood in the house turned very dark. Smo, my mother-in-law, had moved in to help, as had my father. Then one Friday night Weeze got very ill and slipped into a rattling coma, only occasion- ally opening her eyes and squeezing my hand with no strength at all. She seemed very peaceful and not distressed at all. It was as if she was ready to die and was preparing to slip gently away. I called the nurses in as Weeze started rattling, and they came and checked her over. They looked very sad and called me into the bathroom. The two nurses held my hand and looked me in the eye.

'We think you should prepare yourself, Tim, she can't go on like this for very long, and we have to say we don't think she'll make it through the night.'

Too much reality for one person to deal with. I started to weep and all I could think of was how was I going to tell Caitlin her mum had died. I left the room and told Smo and Dave, we hugged and decided it was time to phone round. That night various people arrived: Weeze's sisters, my mum, some friends. There was a general sense of calm about the place. The room was in candlelit darkness and we sat there and whispered to her, how much we loved her, how we were all there for her – how it was OK, that everything was OK. I sat on the sofa in the room and played some gentle finger-picking guitar and sang her sweet low songs to ease her passage. My parents anointed her feet with oil and perfume. The whole scene was very biblical. I couldn't help see her and think of the dead body of Jesus being prepared for the tomb. There was a sense that this was right, that she was going out as she would have wanted, into the next world perfectly prepared. The night wore on and we waited, we held each other, we all wept gently and expected it to happen at any moment. Eventually everyone went to sleep wherever they could and I lay down next to Weeze on our bed and expected her to die with me holding her hand.

At some point I must have fallen asleep. When I awoke it was with a jerk and I checked Weeze – she was still there, still alive. I kissed her cheek. It was morning, she'd survived the night. She had told me quite early on in our marriage that for some reason most people die at three o'clock in the morning, so I thought that if she made it past three she couldn't die that day.

Over that weekend the house slowly filled and every night we waited for her to die and every night she somehow pulled through. Then on Monday morning she opened her eyes and asked for water. She'd survived, made it, and slowly she got stronger, she started drinking and even ate a little. And then she started to talk about her golden bird.

During her darkest hour she had seen her golden bird. It had led her back towards life. It told her that she wasn't ready to go yet and that she had a long time to go. She would make it through to Caitlin's birthday, through past Christmas, she'd see in the millennium and then she'd die some time well into the New Year. No one believed her. Although she was obviously feeling better it could only be a matter of days before she died, a week at most. But she was right.

Something terrible happened, though, over that weekend and it affected Weeze all the way until the end of her life. She felt she should have died that night. She would often lie on her bed and say to me, 'I should have died that night, that was my time, but something kept me back, something held me from going. And I think it was you, Tim.' And she could have been right. As I'd lain there and whispered in her ear, I found I couldn't release her. While others had said, 'It's OK, you can go, everything's OK, you can pass over,' I'd whispered, 'Don't go, please don't leave me, I can't go on without you. I need you, don't die.' Weeze resented me for holding her here and it was something I had to live with and still do. Something broke in Weeze that night. I honestly believe that on that Friday night her spirit left her, but it was her body that survived. And without her spirit, Weeze was a different person. She entered a dark, dark depression. Weeze and I had been through so much that this stunned me and I felt like I'd lost my anchor. Nothing gave her pleasure, she stopped smiling, stopped laughing, stopped being interested in everything and just wanted to die. Sometimes she would rally for a day or so, or if someone came to see her, but when it was just me and her she would say black things that came from a place I couldn't face and didn't want to hear.

Why was I so surprised? Her life had suddenly taken a hideous dive into the extremes of disability. She couldn't wash herself, couldn't feed herself, couldn't even roll herself over to avoid bedsores, couldn't play with her child, couldn't even go to the toilet without help. Several major events happened which I think made it all too unbearable for her. She had various bouts of incontinence, which was messy and painful for her and meant that I had to clean her in ways no wife wants her husband to. She would lie there softly saying, 'Sorry, sorry, sorry . . .' over and over again. But there was nothing to be sorry for, it wasn't that kind of thing. It was just what you did – your job, your vocation was to look after this person and between myself and Smo that's what we did for three months. It was the first thing we did in the morning and the last thing we did at night. It was all we thought about. She had various infections and scares and we were in a limbo land of endless nursing. It wasn't terrible, it wasn't even that hard, it was just what you did. And as Weeze withdrew further and further into herself and became less and less responsive, it became more work-like. I can remember very clearly sitting in the kitchen with Smo and saying, 'Is it just me, because I feel terrible, but I find myself not feeling like Weeze is Weeze, but feel like she's a patient and we're just nurses.' I cried with relief when Smo told me that's how she felt. It was as if you couldn't possibly accept the humiliation of each day happening to the person that you loved most in the world. But if it was just happening to an anonymous ill person, then you could deal with that. And so it went on.

Weeze would regularly tell me how much she longed to die when we were alone and several times she asked me to help her. But I couldn't, I just couldn't even contemplate it. It was selfish really. However tortured she was, however desperate she felt, I wanted her to be alive for me. I could block out her pain from affecting me by just knowing she was alive and that I could still speak to her and touch her. But it meant that I didn't quite see how bad things had got. In one glimmer of her old self she'd asked for a cherry vodka, just for fun. I brought up the shot and helped her drink it. She coughed so much I thought that it might finish her off in one go. But when she calmed down she smiled and said, 'Mmm, all warm on the inside. Can I have another?' I brought up a miniature of lemon vodka and she tried it, but it wasn't as nice as the cherry. I put the bottle down on her table for her to sip at later if she wanted it. That night she had another horrendous night. She'd stopped sleeping at night and spent six or seven hours getting progressively more depressed and frantic about everything. This particular night it all got too much for her. I woke up to hear a scratching and scraping sound. I rolled over and could see her silhouette attacking her wrists. I turned the light on and saw her hacking away at her wrist with the jagged metal cap of the miniature. My first reaction was one of anger.

'What the fuck are you doing, Weeze?'

She looked round at me as if she hadn't realized I was in the room until I'd spoken.

'I can't do it, I can't even do this. I haven't even got enough strength to kill myself.'

Her left wrist and forearm were scratched to pieces, but there was no real damage, and I don't think she really meant to do it. I think she just needed me to know how bad the place she was in was. We sat up and talked for hours, and I went from fury that she could have done this to me, to understanding quite how dreadful her life had become. But the talking and the attempt seemed to have been a changing point and she started slowly, slowly to come out of her depression.

A further knock came when she woke up one morning to find she'd gone blind. She quite calmly said to me as I was pottering around her in the morning, opening the curtains, rolling her over, checking her drivers, 'Um, Tim, I can't see very well.' I asked her what she meant. 'Well, I can't really see at all, some light and shade, but that's about it. I'm a bit scared, could you call the doctor?' She didn't freak out, she just went into herself and dealt with it. When the doctor came out he checked her over and thought that this was probably a permanent symptom due to growth around the optical nerve. I spent most of the day with her saying crap things like, 'It's just another thing, we'll deal with it. You can still feel, you can still hear us. We'll always be around you, we'll read to you, we'll look after you, it won't be that different.' She took it better in many ways than we all did. But we kept going, we took turns to read to her, we changed her, washed her and tried to keep it together. Three days later she woke up and smiled. 'I can see again, Tim, I can see you.' She held my face and looked at me for the first time in three days. I'd thought she'd never see me again, that I was lost to her that way, but here we were, reunited. 'Hello, you,' she said, 'nice to see you.' And that was that – we moved on and the routine kept going. Smo and Dave were around all the time, Paul, Weeze's dad, came over straight after work and sat reading to her for hours into the night, we all ate dinner in our bedroom and tried to keep it as natural as we could.

After a few weeks she was desperate to see something, anything that wasn't the three walls and the ceiling which had become her life. Smo and I decided we could carry her down to the bathroom for a bath. We rolled her on to a sheet and lifted her off the bed into a wheelchair. We then wheeled her down to the bathroom and lifted her in the sheet down in the warm water. The movement and the change of scenery were almost too much for her. It was a stimulation overload. She gradually relaxed and enjoyed the bath, she smiled and even laughed a bit. I got to shave her legs for her. It might not sound a lot but to me it was one of the most intimate things that I did with Weeze during our whole life together. I soaped up her legs, massaged them, and then slowly and carefully shaved them. It was almost too intimate. I hadn't really touched her for over a month, because of her state, and just holding her legs and remembering all the times we'd made love in the bath felt beautiful. 'Thank you, sweetheart, I miss you so much.' At that point I remembered everything, the bliss of our love, the excitement of my passion for her, and how empty my life had become without her there holding me, cradling me in her love. It was a strange mixture of emotions. I felt overjoyed at being connected to her again and yet terribly saddened by the pain of knowing the loss. That was our last moment of real physical closeness. When I look back on it now, I see her in the bath at night with candles lit all around her, sipping wine, though in reality it was in the middle of a dull rainy day. But that's love, it cleanses things.

One of her few pleasures in the last weeks was being read to and we all took it in turns to read bits and pieces. I would read her light stuff from her favourite author, P. G. Wodehouse, doing all the upper-class blustering accents which made her giggle just a little. Smo read her *Gormenghast*, and Weeze loved it, she'd never got round to reading it before. It was the perfect book for her, such strong imagery of a crumbling castle full of weird and twisted characters. It took her out of her own crumbling body to another world, a place so rich in its depth that she could enter it and inhabit it for hours on end, giving her some respite from the pain and the agony of watching herself slowly slip away.

Even in these darkest of times there was something which shone through like a beacon, and that was love. Not just the love that I had for Weeze, but the wide community that grew up around the house. As well as Smo and Dave, Paul was there every day, Gavin and Owen took it in turns to stay in shifts, Lisse, one of Weeze's oldest friends, came down regularly, Weeze's sisters Dee and Jan were always there supporting, as was my mum. Then there were all the people and friends who popped in with pies and biscuits and cards, helped look after Caitlin, and generally offered love at a time when all love was welcomed and needed. In a strange way it made you feel part of a community, all focused on one thing, Weeze, and trying to see her through the last days. I feel an unbelievable debt of gratitude to all of them and I have a love for them all that I would never have experienced if Weeze hadn't been ill. It's that love that keeps you going when your world stops and a blanket of darkness closes around you. The relationships within the house were so intense, forged as they were in this extreme adversity. Two of our friends who stayed with us got it together, lost souls in pain looking for comfort. Weeze loved it! When everyone had left the room she would call me over to the bed and say, 'Come on then, what's the goss? Are they doing it or what?' After a few days of procrastination they did indeed 'do it' and Weeze laughed harder than I thought was really good for her. 'Thank God someone's getting a shag in this house. That's what this place needs, some sex to bring it back to life.'

One day she looked at me and asked me what I was doing about sex. I wasn't really sure what she meant but, ever the frank wife, she asked if I was at least masturbating. I said that in all honesty, with the house so full and her being so ill, there wasn't really the time, the place or indeed the inclination. 'I think you should go and see a prostitute, it would make me feel a lot less guilty about not being able to fulfil you.' That's what I loved about Weeze, she was entirely practical on such matters and never afraid to speak her mind. I told her I was grateful for the offer but that I thought I'd survive. She considered it carefully and then said, 'You're probably right, and knowing how paranoid you are you'd only be worried about catching something, so you wouldn't enjoy it anyway. OK, scrub that idea.' Sweet of her to be concerned though.

The most difficult thing was getting food into her. She really didn't want to eat anything and her taste buds were all up the shoot, so only a few things actually tasted nice to her. One of the things she craved was watermelon. Now, any other time of year this wouldn't have been such an outlandish thing to ask for, but in the middle of winter in Tunbridge Wells, watermelons aren't the easiest things to come across. However, everyone was desperate to get her whatever she wanted and we'd spend hours going from supermarket to supermarket trying to track them down. In the end Lisse phoned round most of the fruit suppliers in the southeast and found someone with a box of them in Rochester, about an hour's drive away. So Paul drove over and picked them up and we had enough melon in the house to last us for months. The pleasure of feeding her food that she really wanted was fabulous, she would make little moans of delight. I'm not sure what it was about the melons that did it for her – maybe her body craved the water – but she would devour the segments, at first with her hands, then later off a fork offered to her by whoever was lucky enough to feed her. And you did feel lucky. I can't explain it and I'm not sure she ever really believed it, but it did feel like a privilege to do things for her, especially if it could give her even a moment's pleasure. Feeding her was one of my favourite things because I was close to her, looking into her eyes, expressing my love for her in a physical way. Once while I was feeding her, a small smile came over her face and I asked her what she was thinking about. 'You,' she said, 'every time you put the fork towards my mouth you open your mouth in time with me.' And she was right, I mimicked her eating action without knowing it – as she opened her mouth I opened mine, as she closed it around the food I closed my mouth, she chewed and I chewed.

One of the things she wanted to make it to was Caitlin's birthday and, sure enough, the golden bird didn't lie, she made it. We opened Caitlin's presents in bed with Weeze and Caitlin looked radiant and over-excited. Two of our friends, Jane and Uschi, had organized a fantastic pirate party in a local hall. We'd chosen it so that Weeze could come with her eye-patch and feel very much in part. We had hoped to put Weeze in a wheelchair and take her down to it, but as the day drew closer this seemed more and more like a ridiculous pipe dream. As a trial run we carried her downstairs in a sheet and placed her in the front room in front of the telly. She hated it. Although part of her craved a new landscape to look at, when she was actually faced with another room she went into a kind of shock. Not moving for weeks on end had meant she'd become far more institutionalized than any of us had realized. We carried her back upstairs after an hour and the pain of movement was excruciating for her – back in bed she relapsed into the peace of sleep for the rest of the day. So on Caitlin's birthday she waved us off, both dressed as the most dastardly pirates Tunbridge Wells had ever seen. Caitlin had a fabulous time and, as far as birthdays for four-year-olds go, this was a corker. Caitlin couldn't wait for it to be over though, so she could run home and tell Weeze everything that had happened. It was a great day for the two of them. Over the weeks and months preceding, both of them, for their own protection, had withdrawn from each other. Caitlin didn't like coming into the room to see Weeze, she wanted me constantly to be with her downstairs, playing, cooking or watching telly. Weeze also wanted less and less contact with Caitlin. I think it was the only way she could come to terms with leaving her. She needed to feel unattached to her before she could leave. She loved Caitlin more than life itself and I think it was this very love that caused her to withdraw – it was the one thing that was too painful for Weeze to deal with. She didn't want any of our pain to be prolonged and once she had explained to Caitlin that she was dying and that she loved her more than anything in the world, I think she just wanted to go, to let both of us start the healing process. But Caitlin's birthday was different, she couldn't stop herself enjoying Caitlin's infectious pleasure. They were back to being mother and child again and for a day I was an observer of their love.

The next major landmark the golden bird had predicted she would see was the incoming of the new millennium. So we assumed it knew what it was talking about and decided to throw a party. Just some close friends, some food, some wine, about five hundred candles all over the house and a truckload of fireworks. It was a really nice night and everyone took it in turns to come and sit with Weeze. She couldn't face everyone at once, but individually it was fine and not too tiring. I went in at one point and found three of her friends, Felicity, Lisse and Ali, sitting on the bed and yabbering away like young women do, slagging off the dresses of the celebs on the telly, swapping tips about sex and men, and Weeze was there in the middle of it. If you hadn't known what was wrong with her you could have been mistaken for thinking it was a group of friends round a bed cheering up a mate with flu. At twelve o'clock I kissed her and thanked her for everything that she'd meant to me and for the way she'd made me into the man I'd become. I then decided to give her her own fireworks. I'd bought some sparklers and lit one on the balcony outside the bedroom to let her watch the pretty little display. She clapped. Encouraged by her reaction, I taped fifty sparklers together. My thinking was, if she likes one then just think how much she'll like fifty going off at once. What I thought would happen was that they'd all sparkle beautifully and cascade little drops of light like a waterfall. What actually happened was a bit more scary. The whole thing went up in a white ball of heat and started melting the lead canopy of the balcony that I'd hooked it on to. I desperately tried to knock it down into the garden to stop a major accident. Weeze kept saying, 'Is that OK, Tim? It looks awfully dangerous.'

'No, it's all fine, that's what I wanted it to look like, pretty huh?'

'Well, I can't actually look at it, it hurts my eyes.'

And she was right, it did. Eventually I got a stick and beat it down into the wet garden below. We were all relieved. I then went into our local park and let off enough fireworks to sink a small battleship. I aimed most of them towards the house so that Weeze could see them until someone warned me that I might set light to the house for the second time in one night and I took the hint and sent the rockets straight up into the air like everyone else does. Despite these minor hazards, the night went well and it was a nice way to go out in fireworks and laughter.

Louise lasted a further week and a bit and then her golden bird came to claim her. From New Year's onwards her mood lifted and she got back to the old Louise that I knew and had fallen in love with. She was interested in things, made gags and generally left the depression behind. It was like a hideous black cloud had been lifted from her. On the last weekend our friend Felicity was staying and we spent the time with Weeze, laughing and watching telly. And that's where it all ends and everything in my life is divided into the Before and the After. I've been writing this in the After and I long for the Before, for the love to be there again, for Weeze to hold me just one more time. She was the most amazing person I've ever met and life will never be the same again. She truly completed me and each day is a struggle to find meaning in the meaningless, to find purpose in the chaos that engulfs me.

12 January

'I have of late lost all my mirth . . .'

Louise died at 1.30 a.m. on 11 January 2000. I missed the last few moments of her life and I can't work out whether or not I feel grateful or terribly guilty for that. On Sunday she became slightly incoherent and started saying things which made little sense. 'I think I'll get up now. Tim, put me on the stage.' Later she started singing 'Wombles of Wimbledon' and 'Come on, Eileen', very English stuff, sorry for the obscure references for those around the world. But then she was a very English lady. We laughed and I said, 'You're not making any sense, you loon.' We both laughed and she said, 'I know, funny huh.' Then she slipped into sleep and never regained consciousness. The nurses were coming in every four hours to check on her and I was waiting downstairs to let them in so they didn't ring the doorbell and wake up Caitlin. But before they got here, Caitlin woke up, I took her to the toilet and on the way back up the corridor my mother-in-law Smo came out of our bedroom and said, 'She's gone.'

And so she's gone.

I put Caitlin back into bed and then went in to see her.

The room felt very lovely, peaceful, released. She was still warm when I held her hand, and she just looked asleep. I couldn't and still can't believe she won't wake up again and tell me it's all been a big mistake or a joke, but I know she won't and if this is a joke then God's got a strange sense of humour.

Her funeral will be on 25 January and she will go out as she lived, with flair. Four plumed horses will pull a glass-sided carriage showing her purple suede coffin — it's all as she arranged, theatrical and over the top. But that was my Weeze, quiet, calm, humble, modest and yet inside her a passion for everything beautiful and extravagant.

I have over the years discussed Hell with various people and Hell I am told is being without God. Well, Hell for me is being without Weeze.

But to the future, she has left behind her more love than any person I can think of and she has left me a life-long legacy of love and passion. We also have Caitlin, who has been very special at this time and is now my reason to keep living, to keep getting up every morning. To say that I'll miss Weeze or to say anything at all really of what she meant to me is, of course, impossible. She was me, and that's all there is. And she still is me, she's just not bodily here any more.

This website meant a lot to her over this last year and I know she'd want me to thank all of you who have come here and read her words. In the last few dark months she began to doubt whether or not it had been a good thing to do. When she was depressed and in pain she felt she hadn't been honest enough with her entries, felt she'd maybe been too positive, but that's what she was for the longest time and where she'd got to again by the time she finally died. In her last week she was laughing again and smiling and back to being Weeze. And for that I thank whoever is Up There.

If I leave it here like this, I'm going to regret it, because Weeze was a funny woman who wouldn't want people crying when they thought of her, but would want people to smile and laugh and celebrate her, so when you think of Louise if you've met her or if you only know of her from this site, then learn the lesson she wanted to be the message of her diary: All our lives are short, go out and live them. Kiss and hug those you love, laugh when things are funny, don't take anything too seriously and take time to notice how great things are even in the depths of the crap that we're all surrounded by. Loads of love to all of you. I'm off to start writing this book I've agreed to about all this and I'm going to play with Caitlin, who currently has a horrific puppet called Peter who seems to be ruling my life. Jeez, he's even got his own passport. Bye for now . . .

The funeral came and went and Weeze would have been proud. It was everything she'd hoped it would be – a true mixture of spectacle and tears.

Now that this book's completed and I sit here reading the proofs a month away from publication, it feels like the last kiss I never gave her.